Grip It and Rip It!

Grip It and Rip It!

John Daly's Guide to Hitting the Ball Farther Than You Ever Have Before

JOHN DALY

with
John Andrisani

HarperCollins*Publishers*

HarperCollins books may be purchased for educational, business, or sales promotional use. For information, please write: Special Markets Department, HarperCollins Publishers, Inc., 10 East 53rd Street, New York, NY 10022.

FIRST EDITION

Designed by Rachel Smyth
Photographs by Leonard Kamsler

Library of Congress Cataloging-in-Publication Data

Daly, John, 1966–
Grip it and rip it! : John Daly's guide to hitting the ball farther than you ever have before / by John Daly with John Andrisani. — 1st ed.
p. cm.
ISBN 0-06-016912-5
1. Swing (Golf)   2. Putting (Golf)   3. Daly, John, 1966–   I. Andrisani, John.   II. Title.
GV965.D32   1992
796.352′3—dc20   92–52557

92 93 94 95 96 DT/CW 10 9 8 7 6 5 4 3 2 1

This book is dedicated to my idol Jack Nicklaus and to Fuzzy Zoeller, my big brother on the Tour

CONTENTS

Color photographs follow page 66

FOREWORD

The PGA Tour has been searching for a superstar for a good many years, but no one player has been able to stand above the rest, as did former greats such as Ben Hogan, Sam Snead, Arnold Palmer, and Jack Nicklaus. Maybe John Daly is the Tour's new Terminator.

Whether Daly will become the man to beat each week on the Tour will only be seen with time. One thing, however, is certain: Not since Arnold Palmer captured the imagination of the golfing galleries has one player been so loved for a "regular guy" personality and a go-for-broke game.

Daly's strongest quality, of course, is his prodigious length off the tee; his drives truly are launched into the air. But greatness can only come to those golfers who possess an equally good short game. Rest assured, Daly has great touch on and around the greens, as I found out firsthand watching him pitch, chip, play sand shots, and putt when I was paired with him in the 1992 Masters, held at the famous Augusta National Golf Club in Augusta, Georgia. Daly finished nineteenth in that Masters, which is remarkable for a first-timer when you consider how difficult the course is and how it takes most players years to get used to its rolling fairways and undulating fast greens. Believe me, as a former winner at Augusta, I guarantee Daly will win there one day—soon!

Daly's fine play since his marriage to Betty Fulford indicates to me that he has settled down to a more mature life-style. And that's good, because to play winning golf, you have to have your personal life in order so that you can be focused on the course.

I'm also pleased that John has been strong enough not to listen to teachers and fellow players who encourage him to change his unorthodox swing to a more classic action. After all, he is a natural and he should stay that way.

Last, I'm happy that John has shared his power and short game secrets in *Grip It and Rip It!,* which I feel will be a great asset to any golfer who wants to hit the ball farther and cut strokes off his score.

Fuzzy Zoeller
Former Masters and U.S. Open champion

PREFACE

I've been on earth forty-three years, and for some reason I have always been suspect of so-called historical facts.

For example, I'll never be convinced that some grown man in his right mind ever raced through the streets of Massachusetts on horseback screaming "The British are coming!" at the top of his lungs.

I still question whether any of our country's astronauts actually landed on the moon; rather, I think perhaps a conspiracy of major television news networks somehow staged this walk, and that the "great step for mankind" was a shot in a Hollywood film studio.

Surely, Marilyn Monroe was too sexy to kill herself.

And long before Oliver Stone appeared on the scene, I thought the Warren Commission covered up the truth regarding the assassination of President John Kennedy.

Of all my theories on the real truth behind historical events, I can only prove one: D-Day really took place in Carmel, Indiana, on August 8, 1991, when John Daly, a little-known, long-haired golf pro from Dardanelle, Arkansas, invaded the Crooked Stick Golf Club, site of the 73rd PGA Championship, and over four summer days single-handedly completed his mission to defeat all competition with his arsenal of booming 350-yard drives, on-target approaches, and deft touch shots around the greens. When the war was over, the rookie superstar had scored twenty-one birdies and taken a total of 276 strokes in all, three ahead of his next rival.

For the duration of this coveted major championship, Daly captured the public's imagination with his carefree personality and phenomenal power game. His puff-the-cigarette pose and go-for-broke game were reminiscent of a young Arnold Palmer; the way he lifted his left heel high off the ground on the backswing reminded the gallery of a youthful Jack Nicklaus swinging; and the way he dropped his club well below the parallel position at the top of his swing brought back memories of the great Bobby Jones, who did the very same thing. As to Daly's downswing technique, no golfer in history ever looked as powerful as he did hitting the ball.

When you consider that Daly gained entry into the event at the zero hour, as the ninth alternate, and didn't even have time to play a practice round over the course's 7,289 demanding yards, you start to appreciate his talent. Even more so when you consider that in the 1991 PGA he beat Nick Faldo by ten strokes, Jack Nicklaus and Seve Ballesteros by eleven, Fred Couples by twelve, Greg Norman by thirteen, and Tom Kite, golf's all-time money winner, by sixteen.

John Daly is truly a rare golfing genius. Which is one reason why I was honored when he asked me to collaborate with him on his first-ever instruction book, *Grip It and Rip It!*

In this book, Daly reveals the inner workings of his very personal method of swinging the club, which ironically is very easy to clone, largely because he advocates things like a strong grip and a long extra-loose swing, which go against traditional teaching but, quite honestly, feel more natural. As an added bonus, he shares his short game techniques for chipping, pitching, sand play, and putting, which you will also find are unique but easy to copy.

Frankly, I think the publication of this book is perfectly timed. Today there are nearly thirty million persons playing golf, the majority of whom shoot in the nineties. John Daly wants to change all that. I think that by writing *Grip It and Rip It!,* he has already taken one great step for mankind.

John Andrisani
John's Island, Florida

INTRODUCTION

Winning the 1991 PGA Championship changed my life in both good and bad ways.

On the positive side, I proved to myself and to my friends and family that I could win a major championship. Consequently, when I raised the tournament trophy over my head, it was my finest moment ever.

I was also very pleased that winning the PGA Championship helped me gain some new fans. I guess they liked the fact that I was an underdog who took a big cut at the ball and hit it far down the fairway. And that, on the way to victory, I took time to stop and talk to them or shake their hands. Some athletes turn their backs on autograph seekers. I have never done that and never will.

Most of all, I was happy that all of the hard work I had done in practice had finally paid off. Of course, I had won tournaments before, both on my home turf and abroad, but nothing makes a golfer appreciate the benefit of the work ethic more than winning one of the game's four premier championships.

On the negative side, I learned firsthand that it's true what they say about the price of fame; everybody does want a piece of you. For that reason, I now choose my friends more carefully. More important, I have learned to say no, which must mean that I'm finally maturing and getting my priorities right.

At this point in my life, I work very hard to play professional golf to the highest standard possible. It is also true that when I win, I choose to celebrate in the style of the late "Champagne Tony" Lema, one of golf's past greats. Golf, like life, should be enjoyable. It is my hope to bring new fans to the game and with the help of *Grip It and Rip It!*, this new generation of golfers will hit the ball longer and straighter than any before.

John Daly
Castle Rock, Colorado

GETTING READY TO RIP IT

I consider myself a very lucky young man, to be able to make a great living doing what I love most—playing golf against the greatest players in the world, on the greatest courses in the world. The thrill of competition excites me, but what really turns me on is "killing" the ball. In fact, I live for the loud smacking sound I hear when the clubface comes into the ball at high speed and contacts its center back portion, hard. The next best thing is hearing the oohs and aahs of the gallery as the ball flies out of sight and finally comes to rest 300 yards down the fairway.

For some reason, maybe because I look big on television, most golfers think I'm built like a football lineman or a heavyweight fighter, and think that's why I'm able to hit the long ball. Well, let me level with you: I'm very strong and very flexible, but at five-eleven, 175 pounds, I'm no giant. Furthermore, more than sheer strength, it's my unique and more natural setup and swing that allow me to hit the golf ball so powerfully and accurately.

While I don't claim that copying my method will enable you to drive the ball like me, I firmly believe that by following my instructions, any golfer can learn to generate more clubhead speed and hit the ball more solidly and accurately than ever before. And when you hit powerful, on-target tee shots, you automatically set yourself up to play a more precise approach into the green and shoot a low score.

Before I review the ins and outs of my swing technique, I

want to talk in some detail about the elements of the *setup* that, if you learn them correctly, will make the golf swing itself feel as natural as walking. I'm referring to your grip, your stance and posture, and the aiming procedures of both your body and the clubface. Also, I'll spend some time talking about the *visualization* process you should develop before you take the club back. I consider the visualization process a very important part of your preshot plan.

THE GRIP: AN INDIVIDUAL CHOICE

As you may know if you've played golf for any length of time, there are basically three styles of grip that are popular for the full shots. I'm going to describe each of them to you before telling you about the grip I use myself, because I feel that golf is a game in which a degree of individuality is important. If a grip other than mine makes you feel more secure when holding the club and more confident that you will deliver the clubface squarely into the back of the ball at impact, then by all means use it.

The first and most commonly used style of grip is called the *overlapping* grip. In this style of grip, the hands are wedded together with the little finger of the right hand resting atop, or overlapping, the index and middle fingers of the left hand. The overlapping grip is also often referred to as the Vardon grip because Harry Vardon, the greatest golfer of the turn-of-the-century era, first popularized it. Today, I guess close to 90 percent of the PGA Tour pros use the overlapping grip.

A second type of hold is called the *ten-finger* or *baseball* grip. In this style, no wedding or overlapping of the hands is involved at all. The right hand simply rests on the club's handle, directly underneath the left, as if you were holding a baseball bat.

The ten-finger grip is employed by a relatively small percentage of professional and amateur golfers. Many golf teachers strongly discourage students from using this grip because they believe that if the hands are not in some way connected, they will tend to work against each other rather than operate as a unit, particularly through the impact zone. Having fooled around with the ten-finger grip as a kid, I tend to agree with this line of thought. However, some good golf has definitely been played with this grip. For example, Art Wall, a former Masters champion, and Bob Rosburg, a former PGA champion, both used the ten-finger grip. So I'm not going to knock it.

The hold that I use is called the *interlocking* grip. To tell you the truth, it was no contest for me which style of grip to use. You see, ever since I was maybe six years old, I have tried to do everything the way my golfing idol, Jack Nicklaus, does it. And Jack is one of the few of the very top pros who use the interlocking grip (Tom Kite, who is the PGA Tour's all-time leading money winner, is another). While I definitely am prejudiced toward this grip because it's also Jack's, I think it truly works best for me and may stand you in good stead, too. Let me describe it to you in detail.

The interlocking grip is similar to the overlapping grip in that the little finger of the right hand again is the finger that meshes the right hand with the left. However, instead of the right pinky overlapping the left index finger, it interlocks between the index and middle fingers of the left hand.

The reason I like the interlocking grip is that the two fingers

A look at my *interlocking* grip from three angles clearly shows how intertwining my right- and left-hand fingers gives me a secure hold on the club.

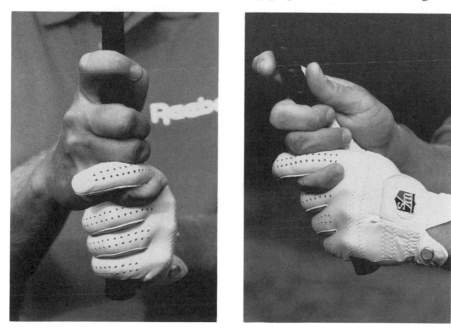
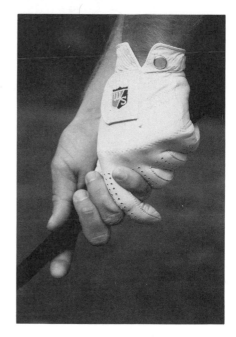

feel more securely intertwined than they do with the overlapping grip. This is particularly important if, like me, you don't have particularly large hands with long fingers.

I think you may have already witnessed how this can work to your advantage on the golf course. Have you ever seen one of your playing partners who uses an overlapping grip make such a poor swing that the clubhead twists at impact, causing him to let go of the handle with his right hand and finish with only his left hand on the club? Well, I find that using an interlocking grip prevents you from losing control of the club, particularly in the impact zone when the club is moving at around 120 miles per hour. Because your right pinky, and with it your entire right hand, is wedded securely to your left hand, your hands will work as a team, thereby enabling you to more consistently deliver the club squarely into the ball. And that, my friends, is the chief goal of all golfers.

REDEFINING *STRONG* AND *WEAK*

Whether you interlock, overlap, or use a ten-finger grip is only a small part of the discussion about how to hold the club. Probably even more important is the way your hands relate to each other, to the handle of the club, and to your clubface and the target.

In golfing terms, for a right-handed player, the more your hands are turned to the right on the grip, the more "strong" you would say that grip is. The more your hands are turned to the left on the handle, the more you would term it a "weak" grip. A "neutral" grip is one that is in the middle ground between the strong and the weak.

For the sake of having a reference point, let me describe this neutral position. First, you would place your left thumb just to the right of the top-center of the shaft—if you'd consider the top of the shaft a twelve o'clock position, then in the neutral grip your left thumb would be at one o'clock. From there, simply close your left hand around the grip, and you'll find that the back of your left hand faces the target, and the channel or V formed between your left thumb and forefinger points just to the right of your chin. When you now interlock or overlap your right hand with your left, you close your right palm over your left thumb, so that the right-hand alignment matches the left. That is, the palm of the right hand is facing the target, and the channel or V between the thumb and forefinger of the right hand also points just to the right of your chin.

Another method of measuring whether your grip is in a neutral position is to look down at your completed grip and determine how many knuckles of the left hand are visible. If the knuckles of your first and second fingers, but no more, are visible, then the left hand is in a neutral position.

What has been termed a weak position is one in which both hands are turned relatively more to the left on the club's handle. Starting again with that left thumb position, instead of it being at one o'clock on the handle, it would be directly on top of the shaft, at twelve o'clock. The V of your left hand would then point straight up at the point of your chin or even toward the left side of your chin. If you were to close your right-hand grip over your left thumb, the V of your right hand would also point toward the left side of your chin. As a final checkpoint to the weak grip, instead of seeing two knuckles on the left hand, you would only see one to one and a half.

Next, let's talk more specifically about the strong grip position. This simply means that no matter whether you interlock or overlap, both hands are turned slightly farther to the right on the grip than they would be in the neutral position. For starters, you would place your left thumb a bit more on the right side of the shaft than on top of it, say in the two o'clock position. As you close your hand around the handle, this means that the back of your hand will be facing a bit more upward instead of pointing directly at the target. The V formed between your left thumb and forefinger will point more to the right, toward your right shoulder instead of toward the right side of your chin, as it does when you assume the so-called neutral position. And you will see two and a half to three knuckles on the left hand instead of two. When you fold your right palm over your left thumb, your right palm should again oppose your left palm, so that the two hands match up—the V between your right thumb and forefinger will also point to your right shoulder.

WHY A STRONG GRIP IS OKAY

If you've studied this game and read a lot of instruction books, you have probably seen a hundred reasons why you must maintain a neutral grip position, with the back of the left hand and the clubface square to the target. The basic thought is that if you start in this position, you're much more likely to finish in this position at impact.

You may also have read or heard through the grapevine that good golfers lean toward the weak grip position, with the hands turned more to the left. The reasoning here seems to go like this: Good golfers are strong golfers, and strong golfers have a tendency to hook the ball. If the hands are turned more to the left, in the weak position, it's harder to move the clubface into a closed position through the impact zone, and therefore harder to put any of the right-to-left spin on the golf ball that makes it draw or hook. On the other side of the coin, most of the prominent theorists say that if your hands are turned too far to the right, in too strong a position, the hands will roll over farther through impact, closing the clubface and putting way too much right-to-left spin on the ball. So whatever you do, they urge, don't use too strong a grip.

Well, let me tell you, folks, all this theory sounds pretty good on paper, but I don't buy it and I want you to know why. First of all, I think these terms *strong* and *weak* are really misleading and they motivate golfers to think the wrong way. Golfers wind up thinking in "macho" terms instead of in terms of what they need to do to hit straight shots. You see, some golfers, especially the better amateurs, begin to believe that the weak grip is sort of the good player's badge of courage. If you're a good player, heck, you naturally hook the ball. Only bad players slice it. So you have to use this weak grip to counteract that strong hook shot.

On the flip side, a strong grip position is often considered by many of the swing experts to be a crutch for a bad swing. In other words, the "weak" golfer who naturally slices the ball might have to use a stronger grip to help him turn the clubface back to a square position at impact, and help him hit the ball straight. Well, as you can probably guess by now, I happen to be one of those "weaklings" who uses what is known, technically, as a fairly strong grip position.

Because I travel to courses all over the world to do long-driving exhibitions or play in pro/ams, I see many athletic amateurs struggle to play golf with a weak grip, mostly because they think it is something they *have* to do to be good. Owing to this misconception, the typical "weak gripper" starts toying with his swing when his shots fly off line, instead of changing the way he holds the club. Before you know it, he does ten different things wrong. I've seen this happen a thousand times. There are gas stations all over the country staffed by young men who insisted they could play with a weak grip.

Luckily for me, I didn't fall into this trap. I may not be too book-educated, but in terms of what's needed technically to make the ball fly far and straight, I'm "swing smart." In fact, I realized straightaway, at a very young age, that a weak grip just wouldn't work for me.

Again, I was fortunate in that I had Jack Nicklaus as a model. Not only does Jack use the interlocking grip, but you may have noticed over the years that he places his hands in a position that is just a touch on the strong side. Not quite as strong as my position, but a little bit that way. This helped me as I was building my game and considering one of the many weak grips I was seeing. I said to myself, "The greatest player in golf is one of the most powerful as well, and he doesn't hesitate to use a grip that's a little strong. There's no reason a strong grip won't work for me, too."

I might add that there is a long list of great players who have come to the same conclusion that I have. Foremost

among them is Lee Trevino; other current stars with strong grips include Fred Couples and Paul Azinger.

WHY THE STRONG POSITION WORKS WONDERS

We've already talked about the theory that is accepted by most teachers and golfers: At address, the back of the left hand and the clubface should be square to the target. They claim that from this starting position, it is supposedly easier to duplicate this position at impact.

Although this theory sounds logical, I have only one major problem with it. I don't believe that returning the back of the left hand square to the target is a natural position, but rather an unnatural one. Why? Because there is a tremendous amount of stress on the back of the left hand in the impact position when it is directly facing the target. The natural position that your left hand would like to be in is one in which the back of the left hand is turned slightly upward, with the butt of the hand leading the way through impact. This position is clearly shown in the accompanying photograph. You can see that the emblem on the back of my glove is facing somewhat upward rather than directly at the target.

Let me give you an image that will help you understand what I'm saying. Suppose you wanted to go up to a door and knock on it very forcefully with your left hand. Would you sweep your arm around and hit the door with the very back of your left hand? No, you wouldn't. Why? Because it would hurt the back of your hand, that's why! What you would do instead is bang on that door with the *butt* of your left hand, because that would give it the strongest blow possible.

In golf, too, you naturally want to deliver the strongest blow possible to the ball, and you will do so if the butt of the hand leads the way through impact. I believe that most golfers will naturally want to bring their left hand through impact this way because they instinctively understand what I've just said. I can tell you from my own experience that I've hit

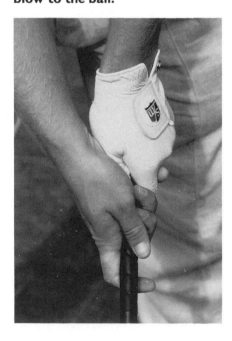

Turning the left hand into a *strong* position allows me to deliver the strongest possible blow to the ball.

thousands of balls using a neutral left-hand grip position, and in addition to pretty weak shots all I got was a very sore and tired back of my left hand. So I said, "The heck with this, I'm going back to the left-hand position that's right for me, with the butt of the left hand leading, the left thumb at just about two o'clock on the grip, and the V pointing to the right shoulder."

I'd like to add here that when I place my left thumb on the shaft, I don't extend it as far down as possible but rather inch the thumb up slightly in what is called the "short" thumb position. This minor adjustment feels secure to me and also, I believe, allows me to make a fuller wrist cock at the top of my backswing.

Of course, as you assume this left-hand position, you should be aligning the leading edge of your clubface square to the target.

I've explained the left-hand position in detail because if you position the left hand correctly, the right should follow. Always keep in mind that you want your right palm to match up with your left palm, so that the V between the right thumb and forefinger points to your right shoulder.

A final point regarding my preference for a fairly strong grip position is that I'm not insisting that you place your hands on the club exactly the way I do. Experiment on the practice tee and go with the position that produces the most consistently straight ball flight for you. Quite possibly you may wish to turn your hands a little farther to the right on the club handle than I do, or possibly a little less. But I firmly believe that the correct position for the vast majority of golfers is one with the hands turned slightly farther to the right than what to date has been considered the neutral position.

GRIP PRESSURE: AN INVISIBLE ENEMY

The position of the hands on the grip has been a basic part of every golf book that's ever been written. Something that's not been covered nearly as often, but which I consider very important, is the amount of pressure you grip the club with. It's something that's harder to see and harder to measure, because what is heavy grip pressure to one person might feel like a very light grip pressure to another.

While my hands feel very secure on the club handle, I can tell you for sure that I do not squeeze the grip at all. Sam Snead used to say you should grip the club as if you were holding a bird. Actually I think that's overstating the case a tiny bit, but I would say you should grip it with the amount of tension you would have in each hand if you were carrying a loaf of bread: tight enough that you won't drop it, but definitely not so tight that you'll crush it.

If you want to reach your true power potential, you've got to grip that club lightly. If you're holding the club any more tightly than I've just described, your forearm muscles will tighten up quite a bit; and when that happens, your biceps and your shoulders will have more tension in them, too. There's no doubt that this unnecessary tension will lessen your ability to make the fullest possible backswing turn and generate sufficient clubhead speed to whip the club powerfully into the ball on the downswing.

Try the following experiment on the practice range, preferably with a friend observing. Take your address position with the driver and grip the club as tightly as you can. Then take a practice swing.

Next, reassume your address position, this time holding the club as lightly as possible, with just enough control that it doesn't slip out of your hands. Make a second swing.

Did the two swings feel different? I'll bet they did. And I'll bet your friend will tell you they looked completely different, too. With the tight grip, your backswing was shorter than usual, and as a result the downswing looked forced. With the light grip, on the other hand, your friend will say that the backswing was not only much longer, but it had a smoother flow to it, with a nice easy transition into the downswing.

I know that I am noted for the length of my backswing, which with the driver goes about fifty degrees beyond parallel to the ground. If I were to grip the club really tightly, I could never swing the driver beyond the parallel position. Why do anything that limits your ability to swing the club fully and naturally? Keep that grip pressure light.

A final point I'd like to make about the grip is the position of my right index finger. I call it my *trigger* finger because it is separated from the other three on that hand, and extended down the shaft. This is sort of a personal idiosyncrasy, I guess, because it feels as though my trigger finger gives the clubshaft a little bit of extra snap coming through impact. Actually, at the top of the backswing my trigger finger comes off the shaft. While I don't do this consciously, I do think that this reapplication of my trigger finger on the downswing adds a touch more speed to the clubhead at impact.

Setting my right forefinger in a *trigger* position allows me to whip the club into the ball at maximum speed.

STANCE AND POSTURE: STAY SQUARE AND RELAXED

To me, there should be nothing artificial in your stance or your posture as you set up to the ball for any full shot. You simply want to put yourself in the best possible position to deliver that clubhead squarely into the ball at maximum speed. What I'd like to do here is tell you how I stand up to the ball on tee shots, then discuss the slight adjustments I make as the clubs get progressively shorter.

With the driver, I advocate a stance that's square or parallel to the target line. That is, a line across your toes should be exactly parallel to a line that is pointing directly toward your target. Picture train tracks, with the right rail pointing directly to the target, and the left rail (the line across your toes) pointing to a spot a fraction to the left of your target.

Even though it seems like a tiny amount of difference, don't fall into the habit of having your toe line aim directly at the target. Although a lot of great golf has been played from this "closed" stance position by champions like Sam Snead and Gary Player, I'd rather see most of you amateurs stay as square as possible or, if anything, take a stance that's a touch "open" in relation to the target line. We'll get into that in more detail when we talk specifically about the subject of alignment.

For now, you just want to know that in the driver stance you should set your feet "parallel left" of the target line. Get in the habit of starting your setup routine from a position a few steps behind the ball. As you step up to the ball from there, always set your right foot into position first, placing it along that parallel-left target line. From there, place your left foot parallel to the target line, then spread your right foot back to complete the full width of the stance.

I recommend that you keep your stance an inch or two narrower than shoulder width. Too wide a stance, while it feels powerful, will tend to restrict you from making a nice full pivot with your hips, something I think is crucial to building power. Think about it for a minute. If your legs are spread too wide and stiff, so they look like two-thirds of a tripod, your lower-body action, if any, will be stiff and rigid rather than full and easy. So with the driver, keep the distance between your heels just inside the width of your shoulders.

One small difference between my stance and that of most of my fellow professionals is that both of my feet are turned out like a duck's, about twenty-five degrees from a position perpendicular to the target line.

Now, most teaching pros say you should turn your left foot out, but that your right foot should remain perpendicular to the target line. The reason this is taught is that when your right foot is perpendicular, it tends to restrict how much hip turn you can make to the right on the backswing. The theory here is that if you restrict the hip turn somewhat, you won't sway your body laterally away from the target on the backswing, which is a fault that causes mishit shots.

The reason I think you should turn your right foot out from the target line is that it *will* allow you to maximize your hip turn. Try it for yourself and see. Take a stance with your right foot perpendicular to the target line, then try to make a hip turn. It may not feel funny because that's probably the way you're used to doing it. Now, take your normal stance and

then turn your right foot out twenty-five degrees. Make a nice free backswing. Didn't your hips and midsection turn a little more fully? Great! Keep that right foot "ducked out" so you can make that fuller turn.

You might ask, now that this adjustment allows me to turn more freely on the backswing, won't I do what the teachers of the square-right-foot position are afraid of—that is, sway off the ball? We'll talk about the swing in greater detail later, but for now, please accept my answer that as long as you make a nice level hip turn around your spine, you can't possibly turn your hips too far. Turn them as far as you can.

Setting up with your right foot *ducked* outward allows you to make the strongest possible turn.

Why restrict yourself? Adopt one of my mottos, which is, *"The farther you turn, the farther it will fly."* Then turn out that right foot slightly, particularly when playing your tee shots.

I'd like to see your weight distribution natural and relaxed at address. Flex your knees just a little bit, so that the weight is centered on your feet for good balance. You should bend just a little from the waist with the driver, but not too much. I really don't like to measure how much you should bend from the waist as some teachers do who say twenty degrees or twenty-five degrees, for example. Just get comfortable. It doesn't take a neurosurgeon to figure out that the longer the club in your hand, the less bend you will need from the waist for your hands to comfortably reach the handle of the club. So you will bend from the waist a touch more with each club as you progress down from the driver to the wedge.

Your arms should hang naturally from your shoulders at address, and really, this factor will automatically determine how far you should stand away from the ball with the driver or with any club. Where your arms and hands hang down to naturally is where your hands should grip the club—this is usually about six to eight inches away from your body. Then the length of the club you're holding determines how far you stand away from the ball. It's really that simple. (Don't fall into the very common habit of stretching your arms out away from you at address. This immediately introduces unwanted tension into the setup and, as I've pointed out, tension inhibits a good turn and square contact.)

One other posture fundamental I recommend is to keep your chin raised just slightly above normal, so that you look down at the ball from the bottom of your eyes, so to speak. This chin-up position will allow your left shoulder to work smoothly underneath the chin as you develop your maximum shoulder turn. If your chin is tucked down so that you look like a turtle at address, your chin will stop your shoulder turn prematurely. Not only that, but because your chin stops the momentum your shoulder turn has begun to build, you can throw yourself off balance. So keep your chin up.

Opposite: **When addressing the ball, your hands should be about six to eight inches** *away from* **your body.**

WEIGHT DISTRIBUTION AND
BALL POSITION

For the driver as well as the fairway woods, I recommend a weight distribution of fifty-fifty between the feet, which will encourage a shallow sweeping action through the impact zone that is very desirable with the longer clubs. You should feel lively, springy, ready—pretty much like a basketball player who is playing defense, waiting for the dribbler to approach and ready to move in either direction.

Your left arm and the clubshaft should form an approximately straight line down to the ball, which should be placed on a line virtually opposite your left heel. This ball position for the tee shot is important because it will allow you to make contact just a fraction after the clubhead has reached its lowest point. Believe me, even I am not strong enough to hit down on the driver and still get the ball to carry a long way. There just isn't enough loft built into a driver to launch the ball high into the air if you hit with a sharp descending blow rather than with a sweeping action. So play the ball almost directly off the left heel and your natural swing arc will actually add a degree or so of loft to the club and allow you to sweep the ball cleanly off its wooden-tee perch.

I tee the ball fairly high for the driver, about one full inch, so that more than half the ball is resting above the crown of the clubhead at address. Again, everything in your setup should encourage a sweeping action with the driver, and teeing the ball high helps you form the right mental picture. Also, with the ball teed up about an inch, you have virtually eliminated the possibility of catching the clubhead on the ground prior to impact so that the clubface is jarred from its intended line. Play the ball forward in your stance, tee it fairly high, and don't deviate too much from this position no matter what kind of wind or weather you're facing. I've come to understand that if you play around too much with ball position and tee height, you make it difficult for yourself to keep a nice consistent flow in your driver swing. In the long run, that's far more important than the few yards you might save

Playing your tee shots off your left heel will promote a *sweeping* hit.

when hitting into the wind by playing the ball farther back, teeing it low, and trying to "punch" the shot. Stick with a consistent positioning and you'll make more consistent swings.

SETTING UP TO THE SHORTER CLUBS

If you're like the majority of amateurs, you'll need to hit your fairway woods on all of the par fives and quite a few of the par fours on your course. So let's make sure you know how to set up correctly when playing them.

The only difference in the setup to the fairway woods as opposed to the driver is that the ball is not sitting on a tee. You should again play the ball forward in your stance to encourage an upswing hit. Also, keep your weight balanced fifty-fifty between the feet to create a nice shallow bottom to your swing. Keep that right toe turned out a little, too, to help you make your strongest possible backswing turn.

One note I'd like to make for all you middle and high handicappers is that if you have what would normally be a three-wood shot, but the lie is a little fluffy, play it smart. Take a four- or five-wood instead, and play the shot from exactly the same address position. With a little more loft in hand, you won't have that subconscious (or conscious) worry that you won't get the ball up out of that fluffy lie. Also, because a little grass may get between ball and clubface at impact, you will get a little bit of a "flier" so that the more lofted wood will give you three-wood distance anyway. Awareness of a small point such as this will definitely save you a stroke now and then.

Long irons are the clubs that most amateurs hate. But the two- and three-irons actually have more loft on them than the three- and four-woods. There's no reason you can't hit them well if your setup is correct and you make a good backswing turn.

For the long irons, assume the same address position as for the wood clubs, except that the ball should be positioned two inches behind a line drawn opposite your left heel. By making this adjustment, you'll contact the ball precisely at the bottom of your swing, which is the key to good long iron play. You don't have to hit down on a long iron as you would a wedge—even I would have trouble hitting a high long iron that way! If you just clip those long irons off the grass with contact coming at the very base of your swing arc, you'll see an immediate improvement in your long iron play.

As you move into the middle irons, there are three slight adjustments you must make:

1. Move the ball back about two more inches in your stance.

2. Narrow your stance width slightly, so there are two inches less between your heels than with the driver.

3. Place a touch more weight on your left side at address, so that 60 percent of your weight is now on your left side.

The reason for these minor adjustments is that now that the clubs have more loft, you'd like to strike the ball with a slightly descending blow, taking a small divot just past impact. This descending blow puts added backspin on the ball to help it sit down quickly once it hits the green. And the narrower stance helps you stay centered over the shot, which becomes more of a priority as the clubs increase in loft. Once you make these three small setup adjustments, just trigger the swing as you would normally.

This may sound a little strange to all you amateurs out there, but to me, the short irons, from the seven-iron through the full sand wedge, are the hardest clubs to hit very well. Why? Because the key to hitting short irons close to the hole is hitting the ball a perfectly consistent distance, and that's tougher for me to do than for the less powerful player. You probably love to hit those eight- and nine-irons because they're easier to hit straight, but they still require care. Let's look at the setup adjustments needed to play these shots best.

The most obvious change is that your ball position is now in the center of your stance—two inches farther back than it

On short iron shots, play the ball _back_ in your stance.

was for the middle irons. At address, your hands will be well ahead of a line drawn straight down to the ball. Also, your stance has become more narrow, with just eight to ten inches of space between your heels. Your weight distribution should be a little more pronounced to your left side—say, two-thirds of your weight on the left foot, one-third on the right. These setup adjustments will guarantee that you strike the ball with a fairly sharp descending blow so that you put plenty of bite on your shots.

There is one other element of the short iron setup that I consider vital: the position of the left foot. My left foot is drawn back from the target line two to three inches. There is a good reason for this "open" position that many golfers don't understand. You see, with the ball back in the center of the stance, the clubface is not only striking a descending blow, but because it has not quite reached the bottom of its arc at the instant of impact, it also has not quite squared itself up to the target line. That is, it will be a touch open or pointing to the right of the target line. By opening your stance so you're aiming slightly left of the flag, you'll deliver the blade of the short irons precisely at the target at impact.

AIM YOURSELF AS WELL AS THE CLUBFACE

Even though my heart and soul are into busting the ball, the name of the game on the PGA Tour is scoring. Of course, you can learn to hit the ball farther if you can increase your club-head speed, but if you don't hit it squarely, more clubhead speed won't do you any good—in terms of direction. There's no substitute for hitting the ball squarely if you want to hit it farther and accurately enough to put a big dent in your scores. So you have to learn not only to aim the clubhead properly, but also to aim yourself properly.

The most important element in your full-shot setup is to align your shoulders square to your target line. The reason this is so important is that in the natural golf swing, you will tend to swing the club through impact along a line that is parallel to your shoulder line. If your shoulder line is square to your target line of address, it becomes much easier to swing the clubhead along the target line through impact.

We've already talked about how to step up to the shot from behind the ball and then assume your stance. Once you've done so, you must be sure that your shoulders are precisely parallel to an imaginary line drawn from the ball to your target. Many golfers have the false impression that if their feet are square to the target line, their lineup is automatically correct. But your feet can be square while your shoulders are either open or closed to the target. If this is the case for you and your setup and ball position are correct, you'll have to make some kind of in-swing manipulation to swing down the line through impact. And believe me, that's where a lot of swing problems start.

The best thing you can do is periodically have a friend place a clubshaft across your shoulders as you address the ball on the practice tee. Then step back from the ball while he or she holds the club steady, and see for yourself where your shoulder line is pointing. You might be in for a surprise. I know that many times when my shots were becoming erratic, I'd use this simple check and find out my shoulders were way out of alignment. Now I've become much more aware of this critical setup factor and stay pretty close to square most of the time, but I still have my teacher, Rick Ross, check my shoulder line. Do the same and you'll save yourself a lot of swing headaches.

Of course, you've got to aim the clubface properly as well. Having grown up with the desire to copy the setup and swing methods of Jack Nicklaus, I do as he does when aiming the clubface. As I step up to the shot, placing my right foot into position first, I simultaneously position the clubhead behind the ball. Then I make sure to line up the leading edge of the clubface with any noticeable object that is right on the target line and a few feet in front of the ball, such as a leaf or a discolored bit of grass. Make sure that as you line up the clubface with the target line, you do it with the leading edge of the club, not the top edge. Because there is loft on the clubface, the top edge can give you a distorted view of where the club is really pointing.

There is one other somewhat individual adjustment I make as I place the clubhead behind the ball which might be helpful to you, too. As I carefully place the clubhead square to the target line, I also address the ball a little bit toward the heel of the club—say, one inch inside the center of the clubface. This is a little idiosyncrasy that is actually quite common among players on the PGA Tour. In fact, Fuzzy Zoeller actually pushes the entire driver head beyond or outside the ball just before he draws the club back. I don't recommend that extreme, but there is a reason I do address the ball toward the heel. As we'll see in later chapters, my hip turn on the downswing is very active, with a big "clearing" move through the impact zone. Because this turn of the hip to the left is so pronounced, my hands are pulled a touch to the inside of the position they were in at address. Because I started with the heel of the club behind the ball, I actually return the center or "sweet spot" of the clubface to the ball at impact.

This is an adjustment that I learned more or less by intuition as I was developing my game in my teens. As I said, it's fairly common on the PGA Tour and I think it's because most of the pros have such a good hip pivot on the downswing. You may not need this clubface adjustment at address right now. However, if you start developing a super hip turn as I hope you will after reading this book, you may notice your hands getting whipped through the ball a little more inside their original address position. If so, just make the adjustment.

WHY VISUALIZATION IS CRUCIAL

So far, you've done everything right and have put yourself in a position to give the ball a real good rip. You've developed a nice, comfortably correct address position and you're holding the club with a nice light grip. It's just about time to pull the trigger—but before you do, I want to tell you about the part of the preshot routine that I feel is the most important of all. That is the process of visualizing the shot you intend to hit.

You know, I'd like to tell you something right here that may sound a little ironic, because you're reading this instruction from John Daly, PGA champ and super-long hitter. I believe that the very best thing I do—better than my setup, better than my backswing turn, better than my downswing turn—is to visualize a perfect shot in my mind every time I step up to the ball. I absolutely never let a negative image creep into my head either before or during the swing. That may sound like a real simple thing. You may be saying to yourself, "Yeah, I always try to think positively," but I doubt that very many golfers truly do the kind of visualizing I do, that's just so darn positive it almost forces you to hit a good shot. So I'd like to talk to you a bit about visualization.

First, let's look at the positive aspects of playing a golf course. Every golf hole has a fairway and every golf hole has a green and a cup. Those are the places you must determine you're going to be. Sure, some fairways are wider than others and some greens are bigger than others, too. But you need to focus on the fairway from the tee, and on the green and the cup from the fairway—not all that other stuff that's on a golf course where you just ain't gonna be.

Have you ever played a different course with someone who knew that course better than you did, who was telling you about every single problem there might be on a given hole? He might say to you, "Now, on this hole, whatever you do, don't hit it to the right—there's a pond just over that hill and you can't see it, and also the wind's blowing to the right so there's even more chance of hitting the ball in the water hazard." You say, "Okay, thanks," and tee up your ball. Before you get a chance to draw it back, this guy says, "Also, make sure you don't hit it in one of those fairway bunkers on the left. They're so deep it's totally unfair. Yesterday I got a bad bounce into one of 'em, then I buried my second shot under the lip and wound up making an eight." By now you're just hoping this guy will quiet down and let you hit your shot. After all, how are you going to rip it down the middle of the fairway when someone puts that kind of negative thinking in your head?

The irony is, most amateurs have one of these negative guys in their own heads. In other words, they do a psych job on themselves! The typical club-level golfer is so concerned about where not to hit the ball that he lacks the mental energy to focus on where he should hit it. You've just got to take the opposite approach, where you see in your mind only good shots landing where you want them to land, on the fairway, on the green, in the hole.

Let me give you a great example of how valuable positive visualization can be; then we'll talk about what you do specifically over the ball. When I went to the PGA Championship in August 1991, I was the last guy to get into the tournament. Actually, I was the ninth alternate, but because of several injuries, illnesses, and I think one or two childbirths, there were enough guys who withdrew that I got the call the day before the tournament started. Talk about the hand of fate! Anyway, I drove seven hours from Memphis, Tennessee, to Carmel, Indiana, and showed up for my first round at Pete Dye's Crooked Stick GC, without having ever seen the course.

Now, most people would have said to me, "You've got no chance to play well: You won't even know where the trouble is and you won't know the yardages." Well, I purchased a little booklet that gave me the yardages, so that was no problem. But you're right, I actually didn't know where the trouble was. And do you know what? I didn't want to know. All I wanted was a good look at the fairways and the greens, because that's where I believed I was going to put every shot. Frankly, I was delighted with what I saw on my first view of Crooked Stick because it was a big golf course, with pretty wide fairways and big greens compared to many that we see on the PGA Tour.

Meanwhile, I believe that all the guys who came in and scouted the course for three or four days wound up at a big disadvantage. Everybody started talking about how long the course was (7,289 yards) and the fact that it would play even longer because there had been a lot of rain. I think Jack Nicklaus was quoted as saying it was the hardest tournament course he'd ever seen. Throw in the fact that the course was designed by Pete Dye, who is notorious in Tour circles for taking pride in "roughing up" the pros, and I'll bet half the field was psyched out before they started playing.

So what happened? Dumb John Daly just kept looking at those fairways and greens and shot a three-under-par 69, playing the course "blind." Then I shot a 67 the second day and was in the lead. On the weekend a really great thing happened—nobody caught me.

The point I'm trying to make here is that without a really positive focus all week long, I would never have become the PGA champion. You have to have positive visualization not only at the beginning of your weekend match when everybody is loose and friendly, but down the stretch, too, when suddenly those little bets and presses have added up and they're all going to be determined on the last hole.

It was the same for me on the seventy-second hole of the PGA. I had a three-shot lead, but there's a huge lake all the way down the right side of this monster par four. One little mistake, a slight block or slice to the right, could spell a quick double bogey. If Bruce Lietzke, walking up to the eighteenth green in front of me, should happen to birdie the hole, the tables could be turned mighty quickly.

That's why most of the gallery was stunned when I whipped out the driver instead of playing safe with a long iron. They thought I was absolutely crazy. But I said to myself, "I've hit this fairway three days in a row. There's plenty of room out there, so I'm just gonna knock it on the fairway again." I went through my normal visualization process, gripped it, and ripped it. When I saw that pretty little golf ball heading down the fairway just like I had planned, I knew I had the PGA won.

THE VISUALIZATION PROCESS AND THE FOUR Fs

Let's go back now to that point in your preshot preparation where you've stepped up to the shot, set yourself square, and placed the clubhead behind the ball pointing directly down the target line. My visualization process really kicks in during the five seconds or so before I start the backswing. Let me explain it to you so you can start using it yourself.

Once I'm over the ball, I think only in terms of target. I've already established my short target, just a few feet ahead of the ball, to which I've aligned the leading edge of the clubface. At this point, if I'm hitting the driver, I focus in on my long target. This is an area of the fairway where I want my ball to land that's really out there—maybe 300 yards away, even farther than I usually drive it. From the moment I take this look until the instant I draw the club back, all I'm doing is visualizing the long, high flight of my ball to that distant target. All I see is that target area. In my mind I never see the hazards that may be at the sides of this nice green landing area—the trees, the water, the deep rough that all the other guys see.

You might be saying to yourself at this point, "Gee, John, that total visualization of *target only* sounds pretty good, but don't you need to be aware of the trouble, which side is not too bad to be on if you miss and which side is *jail?* That way you can favor the better side and lower your chance of getting in big trouble." Well, my answer is that on the surface, this thinking seems pretty reasonable, but in actual practice it will hurt you. Why? Because now you are to some degree visualizing trouble rather than just your landing area. That, quite simply, leads to steering rather than taking a big free rip. I guarantee you that the very fact that I focus only on my target area actually keeps me out of trouble, because it allows me to make my best swing a much higher percentage of the time. I simply would not be able to hit it long and straight as often as I do if I were doing anything except visualizing my target area.

My visualization process is basically the same when I'm in the fairway playing to the green on a par four or par five hole, or on the tee on a par three. The only difference is that instead of focusing on a distant area and trying to hit the ball as hard as I can, I focus on the flag itself, because what I really want to do is hole the shot. It's pretty rare for me not to go for the pin. Even though most of the flags at PGA Tour events are pretty well guarded and are more or less on the corners of most greens, I'm almost always focusing on the flag rather than on the safe side of the green.

I admit that I have the luxury of playing to the pin almost exclusively because I do own a couple of big advantages. First, I probably hit the ball higher than anyone currently playing the game, so my approach shots drop onto the green at a steep angle and stop almost dead. Second, I play with a balata-covered, wound golf ball. By comparison, I understand that most amateurs are playing with two-piece surlyn balls. The wound balata ball carries more backspin than the two-piece surlyn, which also makes it stop faster. So I may be able to stop a ball stiff to a really tight pin where, because you don't hit the ball as high and your ball doesn't spin as much, you can strike a perfect shot and find that the ball won't hold such a small piece of green.

What I'm trying to tell you about your visualization on shots to the green, then, is this: If the pin is reasonably accessible to you, given your normal ball flight with the club you have in hand, definitely put your focus on that pin and nothing else. If, however, the pin is tucked on the front left of the green behind a big bunker, you're a two-iron distance away, and you consistently fade the ball, you must change your strategy. Visualize very intently a shot that starts dead at the flag, then fades naturally so that it lands a little to the right of the hole and finishes close to the center of the green, leaving you with a twenty- or twenty-five-foot putt. This is not a cop-out; it does not mean you are visualizing trouble, but rather the best shot you can play in this particular circumstance.

I think you'll find that on most of the holes you play, you will be able to realistically visualize a shot to the flag itself, and this visualization process will work wonders for your approach shots. It's fun to hit an iron shot close to the hole. As your visualization improves, you'll find yourself doing this a lot more often.

As I'm looking over the target prior to starting the back-swing, I jockey myself around a bit, but it is with no conscious thought about how to swing the club. I guess you could make the analogy that I'm a little bit like a boxer who is looking for an opening, then, once he finds it, sets himself so that he can deliver that knockout punch. I'm sort of moving around, too, staying relaxed but getting myself set to deliver a great golf swing to the ball. As I'm doing this and visualizing my target, I am alternately taking a look at the target and then waggling the club up and down. My own system, which by now I do on instinct, is to take four looks at my target, with three nice loose waggles of the club, one waggle between each look.

After the last look, I'm ready to start the club back. My trigger for starting the club back is to firm up my grip on the club very slightly. Remember, this doesn't ever mean tight. During my waggling my grip is very light; then, after my last look at the target, I firm it up ever so slightly and move into the backswing motion smoothly, with no hesitation whatso-

My preswing routine includes *three* waggles of the club.

ever. From the moment I firm up the grip, I only think one thought, which I guess has become pretty well publicized as my so-called mantra of the golf swing. That simple thought is, *"Grip it and rip it!"*

I'm not telling you that you should copy exactly the number of looks and waggles I take as I visualize the shot, but I do hope you'll work on developing a consistent pattern of nice easy motion prior to the swing, and make it become second nature to you. Believe me, it will work wonders for the smoothness of your swing, and improved results are bound to follow.

I want to conclude this important chapter by telling you about something I use as a mental pick-me-up that is tied very closely to the visualization process which I believe you must develop to hit your best shots. I call this mental gimmick the "Four Fs" and I think about them often when I'm between shots on the course. My Four Fs are *Fortitude, Faith, Focus,* and *Foxiness.* They are traits that I feel are necessary to meet the challenges that tournament golf presents to me almost every day, and I think they are necessary to allow you to perform your best every time you tee it up, too. Let me explain them to you:

- **FORTITUDE:** Golf is not physically tough like professional football or hockey. But I admit it sure can wear you down mentally, whether you're playing for big money on the PGA Tour or trying to win a match in your flight of the club championship. I constantly remind myself on the course to have fortitude, to hang in there, stay positive, and weather the storm that's presented by an especially tough course or the fact that I may not be having a particularly good day. You can't let whatever problems you have had up to the present moment have any influence on the shots that you still have to play. You can't afford to say, "Gee, I'm three down after nine holes, I'm gonna get beat badly in this match," any more than I can afford to say, "Heck, I'm three over par after nine holes, there's no way I can come back and finish with a decent score." The secret is to stay with that pure visualization of a perfect result on every shot and keep making that good free swing. That takes fortitude. Hang in there when the going seems toughest and you'll be amazed at how often the law of averages turns in your favor and the good shots start to flow.

- **FAITH** is a close relative of fortitude. Once you have developed your setup and swing fundamentals, stick with them and have faith in them. The principles I'm describing will work for any golfer within the limitations of his or her athletic ability. You have to have faith in what you're doing, especially if you are in the process of relearning your fundamentals. Don't let a few bad swings, or even a few bad rounds, throw you off the track and start you down the bad road of searching for gimmicks. Have faith in your swing.

- **FOCUS** means keeping your mind exclusively where it needs to be on the course, and that means on hitting your next shot perfectly. You don't have to worry about that hole on the back nine that gives you trouble, or even the next hole, which is a par five that you're hoping to birdie. Neither should you be thinking of the right cross you'd like to throw at that aggravating opponent of yours who's deliberately rattling change while you putt. Or any of the other little aggravations, real or imagined, that come up in the course of every round. All that is petty stuff that losers get all hacked off about and winners ignore. Just focus on your next shot and how you're going to set up perfectly— grip it and rip it.

  You should focus on each shot so intently that when you walk off the eighteenth green, you don't even realize that the round is over. Man, that will mean you've really been focused.

- **FOXINESS** is a term you don't hear associated with golf too often, but I remind myself to play foxy golf all the time. What I mean by this is that you should play the way that you know works best for you, even if some expert or know-it-all playing partner wants to tell you why you have to do it his way.

A good example of foxiness is my attitude toward visualization, which includes seeing only the distant landing area even if there is trouble fairly close by. Let the other guy outsmart himself by worrying like crazy about the hazard, while you just focus in so keenly on your target that you end up hitting it. That's the best way to be "dumb like a fox" on the golf course.

Keep reminding yourself of the Four Fs between shots and even when you're off the course, and you'll find that gradually you'll become a tougher and better player.

Well, we've covered quite a bit of ground regarding your setup positions and your best mental preparation prior to making the swing. Are you ready to rip it? I am, so let's go to the next chapter.

DALY'S DOGMA

Play Ball

Ball position is one of the most misunderstood elements of the setup. The fact is, if you play the ball too far forward or too far back in your stance, it's virtually impossible to hit a tee shot solidly and accurately.

When you play the ball too far forward—say, off your left instep or toe—you will tend to turn your body to the left to put the club behind the ball at address, thereby forcing your shoulders into an open position. This faulty address causes you to swing the club on an exaggerated out-to-in path (rather than an inside-square-inside path), cut across the ball at impact, and then hit the ball off line.

When you play the ball too far back in your stance, the tendency is to turn your body to the right when setting up to the ball, which forces your shoulders into a closed position. This faulty setup causes you to swing the club on an exaggerated in-to-out path, with the result being a wayward shot.

Because a small error in ball position makes a big difference in your shots, practice hitting tee shots until you are confident you are consistently playing the ball virtually off your left heel.

Get Ready, Get Set

If your setup is correct—feet, knees, hips, shoulders all lined up parallel to the target line—your tee shots will fly reasonably straight, even if you make a mediocre swing.

Correct alignment starts with a consistent preswing routine—a series of actions a golfer goes through to ready himself to swing and hit a shot. Too many club-level players hit poor shots because they set up haphazardly, sometimes even failing to focus on the target. Try not to do this. Remember:

1. Form a vivid picture of your actual target that is an area of fairway 240 yards in front of the tee.

2. Check that the clubface is dead square to your target and lined up with the back of your left hand.

3. Jockey your body into the classic parallel position without disturbing the alignment of the clubface.

Keep Your Distance

Many golfers realize that standing too far from the ball with both arms outstretched causes an overly flat swing plane and that standing too close to the ball causes an overly upright swing. Yet, ironically, they don't know what is the correct distance to stand in relation to the ball. If you are confused about this fundamental of the setup, here's a valuable tip: If your hands are outside your forehead at address, you are standing too far from the ball. If your hands are well inside the tip of your chin, you are standing too close to the ball.

Yes, It Does Rain on a Golf Course

Golf is a game that demands that you sometimes change your setup and swing. Depending on whether you're hitting a drive or a punch wedge shot, for example, you will have to widen or narrow your stance or change your ball position.

The conditions of the day of your round matter, too. When the grass is wet from rain, you'll need to widen your stance slightly to promote a more compact swing and play the ball back to ensure clean clubface-to-ball contact.

How to Trim the "Fat"

If you're a golfer who has been plagued by the "fats"—contacting the grass well behind the ball and hitting the shot heavy—on short iron shots, try these tips:

1. Take a practice swing and see where the club contacts the grass. If it is well behind the spot where you have been previously playing the ball, move the ball back in your stance.

2. Focus your eyes on the top of the ball instead of the back of it. This minor adjustment will automatically encourage you to shift a little more of your weight to your left side at address. In turn, this setup will encourage you to make a more upright backswing and clean sharp hit at impact.

Perfect Posture

Correct posture—standing comfortably erect with a slight bend in the knees and waist—is a vital element in employing a good golf swing. Yet many amateurs stoop over or stand too straight at address. To promote good posture, imagine that you are sitting on the edge of a barstool.

Pow!

My buzz phrase "grip it and rip it" will encourage you to hit the ball hard, but it will not hurt to have a couple of other power keys to draw on.

One is to imagine that a tee is suspended in the air horizontally, with its tip touching the back center portion of the ball. Your mission, should you accept it, is to drive that tee through the ball at impact.

A second mental key to promote power is to imagine there is a cap taped to the back of the ball. Your goal is to hit the ball so solidly that the cap explodes at impact.

How to Overcome First-Tee Jitters

A relaxed body and a confident mind are two very important keys to hitting the ball far down the fairway and dead at your target. The trouble is, most golfers become so overwhelmed by the crowd of friends or fellow members that congregate by the first tee that they tense up, think negatively, and hit a bad shot as a result.

To help you overcome first-tee jitters, see yourself making a smooth swing and hitting a perfect shot before you trigger the swing. Show yourself you can do it in your mind's eye. Then you won't care how many eyes are on you.

A Better Angle

The high clubhead speed that I normally generate is a result of a big turn of my upper body and a brisk release action of my hands and arms in the hitting area. However, if I really want to kill one, I make a tiny adjustment in my stance that makes a whole lot of difference in the distance the ball flies in the air.

I simply point my left foot out forty-five degrees, instead of twenty-five degrees, from a position perpendicular to the target line.

Angling out my foot a tad more automatically opens my left hip a little more, which means my hip clearing action on the downswing will be even faster, thereby allowing me to swing the club more freely into the ball at a much faster speed.

Line Up Your Hands Correctly

Golfers who lift the club abruptly at the start of the back-swing are usually very bad long iron players. The reason is, a steep backswing makes for a sharp hit at impact, which is fine for playing the high-lofted irons in your bag, but not for hitting the less-lofted clubs that require a sweeping action.

If your long irons are landing well short of the green and well right of it, you are probably setting up with your hands a few inches in front of the ball. Try keeping your hands in line with the ball or a tad ahead of it.

Go for It!

If you're one of those golfers who gets overly tense when the match gets close down the stretch, forget trying to hit an iron smoothly. If you face a six-iron shot, for example, take a seven-iron instead and hit it hard. You'll find that concentrating on making a killer swing will take your mind off the match, allowing you to hit a great shot close to the hole.

Antifreeze Secret

The typical amateur golfer often freezes over the ball, probably because he tries to recall some swing tip he read about in a golf magazine. When he finally comes out of his trance, he jerks the club away, loses his balance on the downswing, then hits a bad shot. Be like me: Don't dillydally over a shot.

To help you make a smooth transition into the backswing, use a forward press, such as setting your hands level with the ball at address, then pressing them forward slightly and starting the backswing from there.

2
HOW TO BUILD A KILLER BACKSWING

I know that in the past, all of the young "long knockers" who have made a splash on the PGA Tour have been coached by some crafty veterans into gradually believing that in order to be really good players, they would have to cut down their natural swings so that they would increase their accuracy. I'm too foxy to listen to that advice; nobody is going to coach me out of an advantage that many of the guys out here on the Tour would kill for!

Believe me, I'm not trying to brag; I'm just stating the facts. Make no mistake, the ability to out-hit your opponents, at any level of play, gives you an edge.

On the Tour level, what it means is that even during weeks in which my game is not that sharp, I may still come away with a good finish because under normal conditions, I can reach any par five on the Tour in two. So I pick up a few of what I consider bonus birdies, or maybe an eagle, during the course of a tournament that some other Tour players can't expect. On the weeks in which my timing is good and I've got my putter going, I am a definite threat to win the tournament.

On the club level, the advantage of hitting it farther than you thought possible is just tremendous. Let's consider it in terms of sheer numbers first. Say you are a middle-handicap player and that if you make pretty good contact, you can hit the driver about 220 yards. The guys you play with hit it about the same length.

Now let's put you on a medium-length par four, say 400

yards. Suppose you hit a pretty good one off the tee—220 down the middle. This leaves you with 180 yards to the pin— no easy position for someone with your length. You've got a pretty tough long iron shot or maybe a five-wood left to get home.

You've also got to remember something else if you're a middle-handicap player. You're not going to be in the fairway as often as you'd like. Let's take another example in which you again make pretty decent contact, sending the ball a good 220 yards, but you hook or pull the shot a little, so the ball ends up in the rough. Not only do you have to play a long shot from the rough, but you must play a slightly longer shot because you have hit the ball off-line. Remember that the 400-yard distance is measured as a straight line along the center of the fairway to the green. Depending on how far left you've hit this one, you'll probably have somewhere between 190 and 200 yards to get home instead of 180. For you that's probably a perfect four-wood, but unless you catch a good lie you won't reach the green.

So you see, your lack of distance is costing you even the chance of getting home in regulation on many of the holes you play.

THE PHYSICAL (AND MENTAL) ADVANTAGES OF DISTANCE GAINS

Let's take a minute to think about what a realistic gain in distance can do for your golf game. When I say *realistic*, I mean a reasonable percentage of increase in distance with all clubs, obtained over a reasonable time with a reasonable amount of work. You can't get much longer overnight. But as long as you're in good health and willing to work at it, I know you can learn to be a longer hitter with a month or two of good effort.

Suppose you were able to add just 20 yards to your drives. That would be fun, wouldn't it? This increase, which is about 9.1 percent if you're a middle-handicap player, would put you out there about 240 yards. If you've hit the ball straight down the middle, you now have just 160 yards left to the flag. Let's not forget, if you have gotten over 9 percent longer with your driver, you'll also be more than 9 percent longer with your approach clubs. At your old length, you would have been between a four- and five-iron distance from the pin. But since you are 9 percent longer across the board, you're about 15 yards longer from this distance. So you're right in six-iron range to the flag. You're now playing this 400-yard hold with driver and six-iron instead of driver and long iron or lofted wood at your old distance.

I think the physical advantage of increased distance becomes even greater on those occasions when your ball lands in the rough. Your 240-yard drive into the rough leaves you 20 yards closer to the hole, of course. Now you've got 170 to 180 yards left (as opposed to 190 or 200 in the previous example). Instead of needing a perfect four-wood to get home (which would only be possible if the lie were good), you now will be playing either a four- or five-iron to the green. That's a big edge in itself. Remember, too, that your increased clubhead speed will make a big difference in your ability to get the clubhead through the ball, even if your lie is mediocre.

Finally, let's look at the mental advantage of hitting the ball longer. Say you've been playing with the same group for the last five or ten years, and you all hit the ball about the same distance. If over a couple of months' time you were to gain the distance advantage I just described, your foursome match would be a completely new ball game. If you got this much longer, believe me, you'd know you were going to beat them every time out. I know it sounds cocky to say this, but when you get a lot longer, you feel a lot better about yourself and you play the game with a heck of a lot more confidence. It will show in your demeanor, and the way you look at the golf course and want to attack it rather than play defensively. It may even intimidate your opponents.

Add this huge mental edge to the substantial physical advantage that I've just outlined, and I'll tell you what, the ball game's over with your golf group. Of course, you can still play with them, and of course they'll start demanding that you give them strokes to keep the game even. But you can live with that, can't you?

A SECRET TO BUILDING A LONG POWER SWING

Before we get into building a power backswing, I want to tell you a story that I think has an awful lot to do with the power game I have today. And it relates to you and how you can build more power into your backswing no matter how old you are, how long you've played, or how short you presently hit the ball.

I started whacking a plastic golf ball around in my backyard with a toy club not too long after I learned how to walk. When I was six, my father gave me my first set of clubs. Actually, it was an odd set that had been lying around in the garage, and it was a men's set. My dad didn't have enough money to buy me a perfectly fitted junior set, and besides, he kind of thought about clubs like you do about wearing your big brother's old clothes—he'll grow into 'em.

So anyway, there I was at age six, trying to swing a man-sized driver. Not only was the club way too long for me, but it was way too heavy for me, too. It would be about the same as you, an adult, trying to swing a driver that is sixty inches long instead of forty-three inches, and that weighs something like thirty ounces instead of thirteen. And the iron clubs were heavier even though they were shorter, so for me they were just as bad.

The result was, these clubs were so long and so heavy that they swung me. As the clubshaft approached the parallel position that most experts would say marks the completion of the backswing, the length of the shaft and the weight of the clubhead literally carried my wrists, hands, arms, and shoulders around so much farther that I must have looked like a pretzel. It was ridiculous, because at the top of my six-year-old's swing, sometimes the clubhead would actually hit the ground next to my left foot.

Of course, I didn't hit many good shots like this, and probably a lot of golf teachers would have laughed at what they saw. But I believe that a very important thing was being ingrained in me at an early age, even though I had no idea it was happening at the time: My body was being trained to understand what a huge backswing turn felt like. Beyond the obvious loosening effect this clubhead weight had on my hands and wrists, those long, heavy clubs were making the muscles of my upper back, my torso, and even my hips stretch to the maximum.

Just like many other things in life, what is ingrained during the early years usually becomes a habit that stays with you through your adult life. I got used to the feeling of that heavy clubhead cocking my wrists and pulling my entire upper body way around. Swinging a club was pretty tiring back then, but I didn't know it wasn't supposed to be so tiring. I was just having a lot of fun.

Meanwhile, the great thing that was happening in those early years was that my spine was getting exceptionally flexible. Today, I may not look like a great athlete to you and I've been known to eat a few too many cheeseburgers, but I still have the great spinal flexibility that allows me to make a super-strong backswing turn. And that is the key toward developing the newfound power that will make this game so much fun for you to play.

SWING A LONG, HEAVY CLUB

You can either buy a weight-training golf club or make one on your own. Many pro shops and retail outlets sell weighted clubs that are usually the same length as, or maybe a couple of inches longer than, a standard men's driver. The clubhead, the shaft, or both are heavily weighted with sand or lead so that the club weighs about five times what a normal driver

would—four to five pounds instead of thirteen to fourteen ounces.

To make your own weighted club, all you need is an old driver that you won't be using. First, remove the grip (if you haven't worked on clubs and are not sure of yourself, you can always have this done at a local repair shop). Pour a substantial amount of sand or lead pellets down the shaft, then weigh the club. If you are a man who is in reasonably good health and has average muscle tone, a club in the four- to five-pound range should be about right. For seniors and women, it's probably wise to scale back to about a three-pound club.

I recommend that for maximum benefit, you make the club a couple of inches longer than standard by adding a plug to the end of the shaft. A little extra length will add to the pulling effect at the top of the backswing, which is what you want. Finally, put a new grip over the end of the shaft.

Start swinging your training club a little every day in your backyard or indoor workout area. The key thing to remember is that you must swing the club very slowly and fully. Don't worry too much about your mechanics, but rather, concentrate on a very slow, fluid movement. Remember that you're swinging a super-heavy club. Trying to swing it at anything like normal speed could lead to injury.

As you slowly move the club into the backswing, you'll feel the weight of the clubhead and clubshaft working on your forearms. Later, after your arms have passed waist height and the clubshaft has passed perpendicular, you'll actually feel it begin to pull on your hips, your back, and your shoulders, so that they'll want to keep turning even farther. Whatever the length your backswing is currently, the weight of your training club will encourage you to go beyond it. Don't try to decide in advance how much farther you want to swing back than normal. Just let the training club do its work. Then, very slowly and smoothly, start the clubshaft back down, around and through the impact zone. Again, as you work your way into the follow-through, you'll feel tension on your forearms, followed by a pull on your shoulders and torso into a very full finish position.

Start slowly with your weighted club training. Just make

about a dozen slow swings a day the first week or so. Then add a few more slow swings per day the second week, and a few more the next, until you're making about twenty swings a day. You'll find that over time, that weight at the top of the backswing will pull you around a little farther and a little farther. If you continue this exercise over, say, two months' time, you just won't believe how much turn you'll have added to your backswing.

This is a particularly good way to train for those of you who live in the northern parts of the country. Start working with the weighted club at the end of one season and I'll guarantee you a bigger backswing turn and a lot more power the following spring.

THE MECHANICS OF A POWERFUL BACKSWING

To me, the golf swing is simply one big, continuous turning motion. I just keep turning back away from the ball as far as I can go, so that my body actually springs into a downswing turn, which I also make as far as I can go. I use this image of a continuous turn on all my full shots, from the driver down to a full sand wedge. I believe you should do the same.

Let's take a look at some of the particulars that should occur as you execute the backswing. As we discussed in Chapter One, I finish my preshot preparation by taking four looks at my target, interspersing three waggles of the clubhead between them. Then I very slightly increase the pressure in my grip as a signal to draw the club back.

Strive to push the club away from the ball very slowly and low to the ground, straight back from the ball for the first foot or so. You should have the sensation that if anything, the left hand is controlling this initial movement of the clubhead. The reason I suggest this is that any quick pickup of the clubhead, which is usually initiated with the right hand, works against building the wide arc you'll need if you're going to hit the ball powerfully.

You can't take the clubhead away from the ball too slowly.

I know that Jack Nicklaus has stated in the past that whenever he was looking to hit an extra-big drive, he would make certain to start the clubhead back even more slowly than usual. And Jack has always had one of the slowest takeaways in the game to begin with. That should tell you something right there. You'll never hit the ball with your backswing. Just keep that takeaway as slow as possible with the left hand pushing straight back, to give you a start toward the widest possible swing arc.

As you begin the takeaway, you should not make any independent manipulation of the clubhead with your hands. The clubface must start straight back from the ball. A lot of golfers, even a few on the pro tours, are under the impression that they must do something to get the clubhead inside the target line at some point. You don't have to concern yourself with this at all. As you continue to push the clubhead away from the ball, it will very gradually and naturally begin to turn to the inside of the target line. The very simple reason it will do this is that you are standing to one side of the ball. Although we will talk in great detail later about "flat" and "upright" swing planes, for now all you need to understand is that it's impossible to keep the clubhead on the target line throughout the swing. To some degree, the clubhead must move inside the target line as the backswing progresses, and it will do so without any independent hand action from you.

TURN, DON'T SWAY

As my takeaway continues, I focus on turning my right side away from the ball as fully as possible. Notice that I said *turning* rather than *moving* my right side. A powerful, repeating golf swing should always be based on turning as fully as possible around a fixed center, as opposed to shifting the body weight in a side-to-side lateral motion. This fixed center point is your spine, which is the central axis of your golf swing. All of the powerful winding movement we have talked about must move in a circular way around your spine, rather than allowing your upper body to move laterally on the backswing.

The reason I've urged you to swing a weighted club is that in order to make this excellent turn around a fixed axis, you'll need as much flexibility as you can muster. The error that a large majority of amateurs make on the backswing is that they sway to the right. When the body weight moves to the outside of the right foot, you may feel as though you're developing some power to put into the shot on the downswing, but you'll never build as much power with a sway as you will with a good honest turn. Why? When you sway you can't make a good turn around your spine. Furthermore, if your body sways laterally off the ball on the backswing, it has to move laterally toward the target (sway) on the downswing by exactly the same amount in order to make perfect contact. So, obviously, a sway breeds lots of inconsistency as well as a loss of power.

As your hands continue to move beyond your right knee and approach hip height, you'll begin to feel your body weight, which was fifty-fifty between the feet at address, begin to shift onto your right foot. The key to continuing to make a turn rather than a sway is to keep your weight on the inside of your right foot as the backswing progresses. It's easy to let the right knee buckle out and the weight move to the outside of the right foot, particularly early on in the swing. However, as you can see in the accompanying photographs of me, at the midpoint of my backswing, my right leg is still straight, rather than bowed out to the right. About 75 percent of my weight is on my right foot at this point; however, it is on the inside of my foot and will continue to stay there throughout the backswing.

The reason I'm going into so much detail about not letting the weight move to the outside of the right foot is that it's a common problem for power golfers. It may also be for you as you strive to increase your distance. You see, with the low, slow, wide swing arc that you're striving for, there will be more of a tendency for your weight to be pulled onto the outside of your right foot. If you just picked up the club

Turning into a braced right leg and loading your weight on the _inside_ of your right foot is a critical link to generating power.

quickly with your arms and hands in a narrow arc, you probably wouldn't have to worry about any sway. However, this type of backswing hinders your turning action and this plays havoc with your distance potential. So it's better to work toward building a wide backswing arc while being aware of keeping your weight shift under control.

Actually, I can speak from extensive experience about swaying off the ball because I used to do it quite a bit myself. I sure didn't want to sway, but I fell into the habit as I was trying to build as big a backswing arc as possible. And I'm here to tell you, when your weight gets too far to the outside of your right foot on the backswing, where the shot is going to finish becomes a real crapshoot. You may return to the ball just right so you hit it straight; you may hang back on your right side on the downswing, with the usual result being a big hook; or you might end up with the same result I found most often, a pronounced sway back to the left on the downswing, causing the body to get ahead of the ball at impact. The result of this move is a shot that's hit solidly but flies to the right of the target.

If you can keep your weight on the inside of your right foot, you'll build a much stronger coil and your shots will fly straight and far. You'll find, as I did, that you'll need to train your right foot to keep the weight to the inside. Once I became convinced that I had to overcome this backswing flaw, I spent many hours on the practice tee, hitting the longer clubs while making sure that at no point in the backswing did my weight get beyond the center of my right foot—even with a big driver swing. This is tough work. After a few hundred balls, the inside of my right foot, ankle, and lower calf would be the most tired part of my body. I was building up the strength in this area that I needed to hold my weight there throughout the backswing. The effort was well worth it, though, because my lower right leg and foot muscles are now trained so that I rarely, if ever, sway off the ball.

Chances are that as you build a powerful turn into your backswing, you'll also need to work on keeping that weight on the inside of your right foot. I don't expect you to hit as many balls as I do. But if you think you might be swaying or your friends observe that you are, you'll just have to force yourself to let that weight shift only to the inside of your right foot, while still making a very low, slow takeaway with your left arm in control of the club. If, after your practice sessions, you feel tired on the inside of the right foot and lower leg, that's good. It means you're building the strength that will help you make a big turn, yet stay in control of your swing.

TAKING IT TO THE TOP: CONTINUE THE COIL

It may sound as if I'm breaking down the backswing into a number of parts and that there are a multitude of things for you to think about in executing it. Ultimately, this won't be the case. You'll be able to think of the backswing as I do—that is, that it's just one big turn. But I want you to understand the areas in which problems can arise so that you can correct them if they creep into your game. Once you practice the right moves enough after correcting any backswing flaws you might have now, the repetitions will again build the backswing into a single continuous unit.

Now you're halfway through the backswing, and you've built the foundation of a wide swing arc while keeping your weight shift under control. From this point, I think in terms of turning my back as far as I possibly can, so that it faces the target at the top of the swing. Actually, in my case, the upper part of my back turns a little way beyond pointing at the target. That is, my shoulder turn goes beyond 90 degrees, to about 110 degrees with the driver.

There is no limit to how far you should turn on the backswing. If you can turn your shoulders 140 degrees, then turn them 140 degrees. You would probably be able to drive some par fours if you could do that. And, I must admit, you'd also be some kind of freak of nature. But my point is, on any full shot, never limit yourself as far as your backswing turn is concerned. The degree of shoulder turn is the number one thing that's lacking in the swings of most amateurs.

I'll bet there are a lot of you who, for whatever reason, don't turn your shoulders more than fifty degrees in the backswing. It's truly a technical must that you increase your shoulder turn if you are going to increase the power in your swing. That's why I want you to swing a weighted club and do the exercises I recommend in the Daly's Dogma at the end of this chapter. If you currently turn only fifty degrees and find the best you can do is increase it to seventy degrees, you'll see a heck of a big distance improvement. If your shoulders currently turn just seventy degrees and you can get that up to eighty, you, too, will hit the ball much longer. And if you've got a fairly decent shoulder turn right now, say eighty degrees, and your workouts allow you to increase that turn to ninety degrees, you'll be amazed at your power increase.

In addition to your efforts to improve your backswing physically, just knowing that you should turn as far as possible will help you to make an increase. The mind will help the body do what it is focusing on. So keep turning around that spine as far as you can.

As you continue turning your shoulders up into their fullest coil, remember to keep turning your hips as far as possible, in the same clockwise manner. There are some pros who teach a theory of resistance by the hips—that is, keeping the hips from turning while at the same time making the big shoulder turn. The idea here is that you will build up a tremendous amount of torque between your upper body and your lower body, right at the waist, which you will then automatically unleash into a powerful downswing action.

I don't agree with this resisting-the-hips reasoning. Instead, I think you should turn them along with your shoulders as far as possible. First, I think that trying to coil one part of your body fully while resisting with another is too complicated for the average player (or even myself) to coordinate successfully. Second, I believe that the full-body turn ultimately unleashes a more powerful downswing release than the resisting-hips backswing does, for reasons we'll talk about in the next chapter.

So turn the hips as fully as possible. Because of the makeup of the human body you'll never be able to turn your hips as far as your shoulders. However, assuming you have no physical problems and reasonable flexibility, I'd like to see your hips turn two-thirds as far as your shoulders do on the backswing. For example, if you can turn your shoulders a full ninety degrees, then your hip turn ideally would be sixty degrees.

As you're making this full-body coil, your lower body will be in motion, too. Really, the motion in your legs is more or less a reaction to a full shoulder and hip turn.

To promote power there should be two noticeable movements by the left leg during the backswing. (The right leg, meanwhile, remains as stable as possible, holding the weight on the inside of the leg.) First, as the backswing reaches and goes beyond the midway point, your left knee should begin to be pulled inward, to the right, so that by the time you reach the top of the backswing, it points behind the ball (to the right of it as you are looking down).

This inward pulling of the left knee is simply a reaction to the upper body coil. You should not consciously rotate your left knee so that it points behind the ball. If you do notice that your left knee is not automatically being pulled so that it points behind the ball, it's a signal that your upper body is not turning nearly far enough. Don't try to make a fake inward movement with the left knee because that movement, made on its own, doesn't do you any good. Instead, work on increasing that full-body turn.

The second movement is the lifting of the left heel that takes place as you approach and reach the top of your backswing.

If you seek a long swing and a long ball, *turn* your hips and shoulders to the maximum.

If your upper body turns correctly on the backswing, your left knee will be pulled *inward* automatically.

Again, this is a natural reaction to the increased turn you're now making. Because your hips are turning quite a ways along with your shoulders, it will become impossible to keep your left heel planted as it was during the address and take-away. It has to be pulled up by the upper body and hip turn.

Now, I know that a lot of teachers along the way have said that in order to retain maximum balance and body stability throughout the swing, you should keep the left heel planted from start to finish. I strongly disagree with this theory, particularly when you're swinging the longer clubs. Sure, if you determine that you're going to keep your left heel on the ground, you should have a pretty reliable base for your swing. But you will also be severely limiting the amount of backswing turn you can make. And, as I said earlier, you need to make as big a turn as your physique allows. Unless you happen to be Superman, you can't afford to limit the power you generate in this game.

You may have heard of other instructors who say it's okay if the left heel rises on the backswing, as long as it's not "too much." I believe that as long as you keep that resistance on the inside of your right foot so that you don't sway off the ball, it doesn't matter how far the left heel rises. If your turn is so big that it pulls your left heel an inch and a half off the ground, as long as you are retaining your balance, I think that's great. In his absolute prime while swinging the driver, Jack Nicklaus lifted his heel probably about three inches. I'll bet Jack wishes it came up that high now. It doesn't, because in his fifties, Nicklaus is not able to duplicate the huge turn he made in his early twenties.

My own left heel probably doesn't rise quite as much as Jack's did—with the driver I'd say it is pulled up about two inches. The distance the heel is pulled up will be a little more or a little less from one individual to the next, depending on how flexible each person is. The more flexible you are, the less the heel will rise, and vice versa.

Keep in mind, though, as with the movement of the left knee, the raising of the left heel must be in reaction to the upper body turn. It must never be done independently. I see a lot of weaker-hitting amateurs, most of whom appear to be beginners, who make almost no backswing turn at all but who pick up their left heel as they take the club back. These golfers must have read somewhere that the left heel should rise on the backswing, but they sure don't look like they're making a golf swing to me; instead, it looks like some kind of ballet move.

The good power golf swing is not some kind of silly dance routine. Focus on building the maximum shoulder and hip

Let your strong body coil force your left heel to lift off the ground.

turn your physique will allow. Let the left knee respond by pointing behind the ball, and let the left heel rise the amount it needs to in response to your turn, while keeping good balance. If you can do these things, you will have improved your backswing tremendously.

THAT "WINGING" RIGHT ELBOW

We have pretty well covered the movement of your body during the backswing, so now I'd like to get into what your arms and hands should be accomplishing as you stretch the club up to the top and beyond parallel.

The majority of teachers preach that as the club approaches the top of the backswing, your arms should remain relatively tight to your body. They suggest that your hands and arms should remain in a rather low position, with your firm left arm remaining at or below the angle at which your shoulders have turned away from the ball. When your left arm is in this position, they note, your right arm will be very much tucked in to your right side, with the right elbow pointing more or less down. A checkpoint that these theorists like to use is that if you are in what is often termed a "connected" position, you would be able to place a handkerchief underneath your right armpit and make a complete backswing without the handkerchief dropping out.

If you look at the accompanying rear-view photograph of my backswing, you may note that I've swung my arms on a plane that would be considered upright. That is, my arms have swung above the angle on which my shoulders have turned, so that at the very top of the swing my hands are more above my head than they are behind me.

In a minute, I'll tell you why I try to reach for this upright

Swinging your arms *high* will allow you to whip the club down into the ball at high speed and make a more direct hit at impact.

position and why I think it will benefit you. For now, let me tell you how to reach it.

As I'm making that full turn with my body, I simply tell myself to reach for the sky with my hands. This reaching sensation is quite simple to achieve if you take the club away as I recommended, straight back from the ball, low to the ground, and with your left hand and arm controlling the action. To some degree your body build will determine how high or upright you can swing your hands—the tall player who stands closer to the ball at address can naturally make a more upright backswing than the shorter player. However, I'm under six feet tall and I manage to make a very upright arm swing, so it definitely can be done. Just turn your body as fully as you can as you push your hands and arms upward toward the sky.

I'd like to point out one other thing that occurs when you execute this upright arm swing. My right elbow is more up and away from my body than it is in that tucked-in position that many teachers advocate. Instead of pointing down, the elbow points pretty much behind me. And no, I definitely can't hold a handkerchief under my arm at the top of the backswing. But let's leave the magic tricks to others and do what we can to help you hit good golf shots.

This "flying" or "winging" right elbow is the source of a lot of controversy in the golf swing. It's been stated many times that a winging elbow means that the swing is not on plane, that it's too upright. Well, I just don't buy the theory that there is one perfect plane on which everybody ought to swing the club. Ben Hogan swung the club on a plane that even the perfect-plane theorists would have said was too low or too flat. While I don't like a flat plane, either, I understand Hogan was a pretty good player.

Of course, early in his career my role model, Jack Nicklaus, had a really upright swing. His right elbow winged out more than mine does today. I understand that Jack was really taken to task for this apparent flaw. However, Jack "only" managed to win eight major championships by the time he was twenty-six, so that quieted a lot of people. And it proved that

To promote a strong, upright swing, push your hands toward the *sky* at the top of the backswing.

his upright swing worked. Here are two big reasons why I think it will work for you:

1. The more upright arm swing will keep the club moving more along the target line than will the flatter swing. The flatter the swing, the more important it will become that the clubhead contact the ball at the precise moment at which it is traveling parallel to the target line. This flatter swing makes it all the more important that your ball position at address be perfect—if it's too far back, you'll push the shot, and if it's too far forward, you'll pull it. When you deliver the clubhead from a more upright angle, it won't matter as much whether your ball position is perfect, because the clubhead is not deviating as much from a path that's more along the target line.

2. I think it's a very much overlooked fact that the upright arm swing will make you a much more effective player out of the rough. Any swing plane can be effective when you're hitting the ball from a good lie in the fairway. But the upright swing gives you a big edge when you miss the fairways. The reason is, when your club approaches the ball from this more upright angle, there's less chance that long grass can wrap around the hosel of the club and slow its momentum, muffling the shot. Also, with the upright swing, less grass intervenes between the clubface and the ball at impact so that you can impart more backspin and control to your shots.

It's important to be realistic about what type of swing you need in order to work your ball around the golf course most effectively. Most amateurs don't realize that they're hitting a heck of a lot more shots from the rough than they are from the fairway. Look at it this way. Even the most accurate drivers on the PGA Tour hit only 70 to 75 percent of the fairways. The less accurate drivers on the Tour hit maybe 55 to 60 percent of the fairways. So be realistic. How many fairways can you expect to hit per round?

Sure, you'd like to hit as high a percentage as you can, and

Letting the right elbow *fly* on the backswing is a must for a solid, upright action.

I think after you begin to apply the principles provided here, you will hit more fairways because you'll be hitting the ball more squarely. But it pays to realize that you're going to be in the rough sometimes. Therefore, the upright arm swing will really help you hit more greens from the rough. It will also at least ensure that you'll get the ball out of deep grass and advance it farther than you possibly could have with a flatter swing. Looking at it over the course of a season, you just won't believe how many strokes this added capability will save you when playing from the deep stuff.

So strive to get your hands high at the top of your swing

and don't pay any mind to whether you're winging that right elbow.

CROSSING THE LINE: WHY IT'S OKAY

Suppose you've done everything I've suggested so far and have made a much-improved, more wound-up, fuller backswing. You may be thinking that you're really ready to "rip it," and in reality you are. However, here again you may be in for some criticism from any standard swing theorists you play with, who may now point out to you that you're "crossing the line" at the top of your backswing.

First, let me explain what the term *crossing the line* means. Second, I'll tell you why it often occurs (naturally) in the full-turn golf swing. And third, I want to state my case as to why it's all right for you to cross the line.

At the top of your backswing the clubshaft is on the line if it's pointing exactly parallel to the target line. Generally this is considered to be the most desirable position to be in, under the premise that there's no need to manipulate the club on the downswing to produce a square hit.

If your club were to point to the left of the target at the top of the backswing, you'd be in what is termed a "laid-off" position. Not too many teachers would favor this position because when your clubshaft is pointing to the left of target, it means that your hands are somewhat closer to the target line than you'd like them to be, and the clubhead is farther away from it (more to the left). From this position, it's easy for your right shoulder and your hands to come over the ball from the outside in. This usually results in a slice, although for the better golfer it's often a pull or pull-hook. However, the results are never carved in stone. Ben Hogan played from a slightly laid-off top-of-backswing position and hit the ball awfully well.

Now, if your clubshaft crosses or points to the right of the target line at the top, you are crossing the line. It's been argued that the path of the club on the downswing will tend to mirror the line the clubshaft is pointing toward at the top, so if anything, you are likely to swing through the ball from the inside out. This starts the ball to the right of the target line and usually puts a right-to-left spin on the ball so that a draw or a hook will result.

If you were to look at the top-of-swing positions of today's top pros from behind the target line, you would notice that the majority of them, including myself, cross the line. And this isn't too surprising because as you probably know, most Tour players can draw the ball easily—partly because they get into this position at the top.

If you _cross_ the line like I'm doing here, hitting a power draw shot will be easy.

There are two reasons why I think it's okay that you cross the line at the top, beyond the simple fact that I and many other pros cross the line. First, I think that the longer the backswing you can make, the greater the likelihood that your clubshaft will naturally cross the target line. And since I'm advocating that you develop the biggest possible turn and the longest backswing you can, crossing the line is just a natural result of accomplishing this. Second, the more upright an arm swing you make, the more likely you are to cross the line a bit at the top. That's because in an upright swing, the right elbow flies away from the body, and when it does, the hands turn to the right in relation to the target line. Since the hands are holding onto the club, this also automatically points the clubshaft more to the right in relation to the target line—in the classic cross-the-line position. Now that I've explained all this, I want to remind you to go back and stick to the backswing principles I've outlined earlier in this chapter. You don't have to worry about whether you're crossing the line or not. The clubshaft will naturally take care of itself.

KEEP WRISTS LOOSE AT THE TOP

The last backswing point I'd like to talk about is the positioning of your wrists at the top. Actually, I'm not as much concerned with the positioning as I am that you keep them loose and relaxed, because this will naturally add power to your shots.

As I've said, very few people can match the length of my backswing. That's primarily true because of the tremendous body turn I make. It's also partly true because I've been blessed with very supple wrist joints and I make the most of them by allowing my wrists to cock to the max at the very top of the swing.

When I say "cocking the wrists," I'm referring to an upward movement of the wrists, while holding your hands in front of you with the palms facing one another. Don't confuse cocking of the wrists with any side-to-side hinging that you can also do from this hands-in-front, palms-together position.

When this cocking motion is allowed at the top of the backswing, the wrists are actually cocking downward because your hands are now above and behind you. Of course, as the wrists cock down, the clubshaft angles down quite a few degrees more than it would if the wrists remained stiff. An extra ten degrees of wrist cock would mean that the clubhead will travel a much longer distance as the backswing completes itself.

Naturally, some golfers can produce a greater degree of wrist cock than others. Again, my own wrists happen to be pretty flexible and so they cock downward quite a bit, adding

Cocking your wrists *downward* at the top of your swing will program added power into your drives.

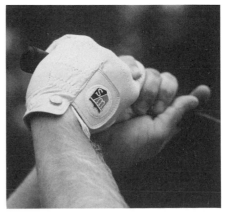

greatly to the length of my backswing with the driver. Even if you can't cock your wrists this much, it will help to remind yourself to keep your grip pressure light on the club at all points of the swing, including at the top. Don't try to control the club's position at the top with additional pressure from your hands.

With a full turn of the shoulders and hips, a nice high arm swing, good balance with most of your weight staying to the inside of your right foot, and a nice light grip that lets the club hang freely at the top, you're in a great position to give the ball a bigger rip than even you might have thought possible. With that in mind, let's see just what's needed on the downswing to complete a dynamic full-swing package.

DALY'S DOGMA

Sway Prevention

Moving the body away from the target laterally on the backswing in such an exaggerated fashion that weight shifts to the outside of your right foot is a common fault of amateur golfers that leads to mishit shots.

If a friend has told you that you have this problem or you have seen yourself sway on video, practice hitting shots with a golf ball lodged under the right side of your instep. This will encourage you to keep your weight on the inside of your right foot during the backswing, which is exactly where it should be to ensure that you stay steady over the ball and coil into a braced right leg.

Forget the Parallel At-the-top Position

I'm not a historian of golf instruction; however, I'd sure like to scold the teacher or professional who first advised a student to swing the club back to the parallel position (clubshaft parallel to the target line at the top of the backswing). It also bugs me that some modern-day teachers have called this the "classic" position.

Trying to arrive and stop in the parallel position at the top is so hard to do that it causes the player to lift the club on too steep an angle or to pause so long at the top that he finds it very difficult to make a smooth transition into the downswing.

Don't worry if you go beyond the parallel position. Just tell your teacher John Daly said it was all right.

Lift Off

Many golfers over fifty years of age lack the flexibility of younger players. Yet some seniors who don't accept this fact try to make a big swing, resulting in back injuries. Consequently, they must put their game on hold or, in some cases, quit.

You don't have to quit golf. Furthermore, you don't have to stop trying to make the big swing, provided you stop staying flat-footed during the motion. That's what's causing you to feel tight.

Let your left heel lift off the ground on the backswing as you turn your body, and see how much bigger your backswing becomes.

Let Your Left Arm Bend

One of the myths of golf instruction is that you must keep your left arm stiff during the backswing. Now wonder so many golfers can't swing the club back far enough and look so robotic. All this advice does is cause the golfer to tense up, and when you're tight you can't generate sufficient clubhead speed to bring the club powerfully into the ball at impact.

Many of the greatest names of the past and some of today's living legends allow the left arm to bend. I know I do; it puts an added springiness in my hands and wrists and allows me to catapult the club into the ball on the downswing. So the next time you go out to practice or play, allow your left arm to bend as late as possible on the backswing.

The Proper Path

The most common takeaway faults are pulling the club back on an exaggerated inside path or pushing it back on a path well outside the target line.

The proper path for the club to swing along initially is straight back along the target line. To help you start the club on the proper path, imagine that you're dragging it through a foot-long trough of molasses that starts behind the ball and extends back along the target line.

Right Your Reverse

If you "reverse pivot"—tilt your weight toward the target on the backswing, then rock it back away from the target on the downswing—you're probably moving your head toward your shoulder instead of keeping your head still and waiting for your left shoulder to rotate under your chin. Bear in mind that your head weighs about twenty pounds, so if you move it toward the target, it's no wonder your weight shifts improperly to the left side on the backswing.

To help you keep it steady and shift your weight correctly to your right side, focus your eyes on a spot directly behind the ball and stare intently at it until your left shoulder brushes your chin.

Turn Your Back on the Target

Coiling the upper body like a spring on the backswing is a critical link to power and a vital part of the swing's chain reaction. The more wound up you are, the faster your uncoiling action on the downswing. The faster your uncoiling action, the faster the speed of the clubhead. The faster the speed of the clubhead, the farther the ball travels.

The weekend golfer has so many technical thoughts in his

head that he gets confused on how to trigger the windup action. If you do, too, this tip should allow you to more easily coil your upper body like a pro: Turn your back to your target.

Get Physical, Get Flexible

Before your weekend round or rounds, here are a few simple exercises I strongly recommend you get in the habit of doing before you head out to the course. I do these exercises, as do Jack Nicklaus and other top professionals, for the simple reason that they enable you to stretch and loosen your stiff muscles and therefore enhance your body coil.

- **TOE TOUCHES.** You can do these either from a standing position or sitting on the floor with your legs stretched out in front of you. I usually do them sitting on the floor, with my feet roughly shoulder width apart.

  Start by stretching both arms slowly toward your left big toe, and try to reach your left toe with the fingers of both hands. If you can't reach it, fine—just extend your fingers as far as you can and hold them there for a few seconds before relaxing back from that stretched position. Next, reach your fingers toward your right big toe as far as you can, holding that stretched position for about five seconds, then relax.

  Repeat this stretch-and-hold exercise. You may notice that on the second go, you're able to reach about an inch farther toward your toes than you did on the first shot, which means your spine is starting to limber up.

  Repeat this exercise a third and final time. You might find your fingers reaching a tad farther still this time around. Remember to hold the stretched position, rather than bouncing in an attempt to reach farther, as holding the position will prevent you from straining a muscle.

- **THE "CRUNCH."** Having just stretched the spine out, stretch your spine in by doing the following: From the position on the floor where you just finished stretching, draw

your knees up and in, as close to your chest as possible. Then wrap your arms around your knees; and with your head down, "crunch" yourself in as tightly as possible, holding that position for at least five seconds.

- **SIDE BENDS.** Lie down on the floor with your feet flat on the ground and your knees up. Place your arms at your side in a relaxed position with the palms down. Now slowly turn your knees to the left. Try to make your left knee reach the floor while keeping your back, shoulders, and hands flat on the floor.

   You'll find that in trying to reach the floor with your knee, your right shoulder and your right hand will want to pull away from the flat positions. Keep your back and your right hand flat. Just work your legs (and with them, your hips and midsection) as far to the left as possible and hold that position for three seconds. Then swing your knees slowly in the opposite direction, trying to reach the floor with your right knee, while keeping your left upper back and your left hand flat on the floor. Hold this stretch for three seconds.

   Repeat these side bends for a total of five minutes in each direction.

When you finish this brief set of exercises, I recommend that you take a hot shower. Let me tell you why.

A couple of years ago I read an article about Kevin Mitchell, the baseball slugger on the Seattle Mariners team, who is annually at or near the top of the major league home run list. In this article, Mitchell said he had adopted the habit of taking a hot shower before each game. He believed that a steady ten-minute burst of warm water hitting his back and neck muscles really relaxed him, with the result that his baseball swing was noticeably looser and more flowing during the game that followed. And, as you will see throughout this book, I'm in favor of anything that promotes smooth rhythmic movements in the golf swing. So do what I do: Follow Mitchell's advice and you'll find it very helpful to the flow of your golf swing.

JOHN DALY'S KILLER SWING

FACE-ON VIEW

Address

Takeaway

At the Top

Impact   **Follow-through**

Finish

DOWN-TARGET VIEW

Address

Takeaway

At the Top

Impact   **Follow-through**

Finish

3
GO AHEAD
AND RIP IT!

We've almost reached the moment of truth, that vital instant when clubface meets ball and you either watch your shot soar high, straight, and long—or gape in dismay as the ball veers quickly off course and leaves you in trouble. Believe me, if you have ingrained the correct posture and alignment techniques and have put yourself in position with a great backswing turn, you are ninety percent along toward hitting an excellent power shot.

There's not an awful lot you have to think about in order for your downswing, impact position, and follow-through to be top-notch. The downswing happens so fast, there isn't time to do much thinking. More than anything, I believe it's important for all golfers to maintain an aggressive mind-set as they bring the club down and through the hitting zone.

As a worldwide golf traveler, I see many amateur golfers who, for one reason or another, just do not seem to be aggressive through the ball. Have you ever noticed players like these? They look like pros as they analyze the shot, set up to the ball, and make a beautiful, flowing backswing. Then, I don't know why this happens, but they seem to try to push or steer the clubhead through the impact zone, rather than use the good turn they've made and freewheel through the ball. The result is a definite loss of clubhead speed and poor point of impact, so they not only lose distance but hit the ball wildly, too. Short, wild tee shots are a disadvantage you just can't make up for.

You frequently hear about golfers who are plagued with so much fear on the putting greens that they develop the "yips." That is, they can't draw the putterblade back from the ball and stroke smoothly through it so that the blade stays on the target line. It's pretty much agreed that the yips are caused by

The one thought that will help you come into impact more aggressively and hit through the ball powerfully, as I'm doing here, is "let it rip."

a lack of confidence that golfers develop over a long period of time, until they eventually believe that something bad is going to happen whenever the putter is drawn back. They get so nervous that they flinch instead of accelerating through the putt in the same way they should on a full shot.

I mention this because I believe that a good many golfers, whether they know it or not, have a case of the yips with the driver. Probably because of bad mechanics over the years, they've watched an awful lot of tee shots sail either out of bounds, into water hazards, or into the trees. They realize that their driver swing is costing them quite a few shots per round and they are concerned enough that it really bugs them. After a while, they become so anxiety-ridden that they make a short, tense backswing, then sort of stab at the ball on the downswing, just like the yipper does on the greens. The ball might be smothered, sliced, popped up, topped—anything but hit solid and straight.

I can't prove that even good golfers can yip their drives, but experience tells me it happens often. Otherwise, how come so many players hit great-looking drives on the practice tee, but suddenly start hitting the ball all over the golf course? They just aren't swinging through the ball with the nice, smooth, freewheeling action they're capable of.

So before we get into the few simple downswing moves that will help you hit the ball long and straight, I'd like to urge you to change your attitude about driving, particularly if you're one of those closet yippers with the long stick. Stop being so damn nervous about where you don't want the ball to go, and within the boundaries of maintaining good balance, give the darn ball a good rip.

Driving the ball should be a lot of fun. It might help your confidence to think of the driver as an "area" club rather than a precision club. You don't have to stop the ball on a dime like you do with a wedge to a tight pin position. Instead, on most holes, you have a fairway that's about forty yards wide. Plus, on the majority of holes, you have ten or more yards of open rough on either side of the fairway that, once you've built more power into your swing, really shouldn't be that much of a concern. So that's usually about sixty yards of space for you to hit your 1.68-inch ball into. You'll accomplish this goal if you trust your swing.

PLANT THE LEFT HEEL

You've put yourself in a strong, fully coiled position at the top. Your shoulders should be turned at least ninety degrees with a hip turn of about sixty degrees, you're holding that shifted weight on the inside of your right foot, and your wrists are nice and loose at the top so that the clubhead is hanging nicely.

Now put the downswing into gear with one simple move—slam your left heel firmly back down into the ground.

This one simple move practically guarantees a good aggressive move into and then through the ball. The reason? You've built up a great deal of tension in that complete body coil at the top. By literally slamming that left heel back down, you have stretched the left side of your body so much that you are virtually forced to swing the club down. There's so much tension in your left side at this instant that you couldn't hold yourself in this position if you wanted to. A release of the entire body in the proper sequence of motion *must* follow. Your left-heel slam pulls down your left leg and hip, your left hip pulls on your midsection, your midsection pulls on your shoulders, and your shoulders pull on your arms. Last, your arms will pull on your hands and your hands will begin to bring the clubhead downward from the top-of-the-swing position, with the clubhead approaching the ball from inside the target line.

Now, remember, you don't have to make your various body parts do all the things I just mentioned. If you have built enough lively tension into your backswing, then when you slam down your left heel, the power you will generate literally can't be stopped. That's the beauty of it—the downswing basically becomes a reaction rather than a planned delivery of the clubhead. And you know, I think it's actually good to make a "brain-dead" downswing, rather than one in which you're trying to think the club into the ball. Because once you slam that left heel down to commence the downswing, there's too little time left to do much thinking anyway.

As I illustrate here, replanting your *left heel* at the start of the downswing will automatically allow your club to achieve maximum speed in the hitting area.

KEEP CLEARING THE HIPS

There is another important movement I'd like you to be aware of that you should make certain you're accomplishing throughout the downswing. The move I am referring to is a very level, counterclockwise turning of your hips throughout the downswing. That is, your hips continue to move around in a circular fashion, to the left, on the downswing, just as they turned in a circular fashion to the right on your back-

swing. You may already be executing this move perfectly and if that's the case, fine. If not, a little change in your perception of your lower-body movement can enhance your release at impact.

It's a mistaken opinion that at impact you should look just like you did at address. As I'll explain in a moment, if your hips return to a square position at impact, it will cause you problems. At any rate, by impact my hips will have turned at least fifty degrees around or to the left of that square position they were occupying prior to the takeaway.

You're probably wondering why the hips should turn this far. There are three good reasons. First, a full, ongoing counterclockwise hip turn continues and indeed increases the release momentum you started by slamming down the left heel. The end result of the chain reaction of this body pull is that the clubhead will continue to accelerate through and beyond impact.

A second benefit is that continuing to lead the downswing with the movement of your lower body assures you that your hands and arms will remain the last link in the release chain. So, there will be no urge for you to make the mistake of trying to create power with your shoulders, arms, and hands. Such an incorrect perception almost guarantees that you will throw the shoulders and arms, and with them the club, outside the swing plane you took the club back on; for the average golfer, this move almost ensures a weak, sliced shot. Again, keeping a continuous counterclockwise turning of the hips going will eliminate any feeling that you need to hit with your upper body.

Third, and I think most important, the reason you must keep your hips actively clearing to the left is that you give your hands and arms the needed space to fully release through impact.

Take a close look at the accompanying photograph of me coming into the ball. Can you see how my arms and hands are approaching the ball from inside the target line, yet my hands have plenty of room to work past my body? When you're in this position, your hands can make a complete release, and a complete release is necessary for you to square up the club at impact.

Many golfers who have the capability to give the ball a good ride cheat themselves out of power because they don't make a good circular hip turn on the downswing. Instead, they make too much of a hard lateral hip slide toward the target. Instead of turning the left hip to the left, they drive it laterally well beyond the point it occupied at address. This feels like a powerful move, but the fact is, if the left hip

Clearing your hips allows you to approach the ball correctly from inside the target line and release your hands, arms, and club more freely.

doesn't clear, then the lower body blocks the hands from releasing the club at impact. The hands can't release the clubhead so that it moves as it should, from inside the target line prior to impact, onto the target line at impact, and then back to inside the target line after impact. Instead, the arms, hands, and clubhead approach the ball from inside the line, but instead of squaring up and then moving back to the inside, the hands (and with them the clubhead) are forced to continue to move from the inside out. So the clubhead path through the ball will start the ball to the right of the target.

Another flaw that the exaggerated lateral hip slide creates

is that, in addition to the altered swing path, the clubface itself will remain open to the target line at impact. The reason? The clubface will naturally square itself to the target line at a point when it's in the same relationship to your body that it was in at address. If your left hip and side are, say, six inches to the left of where they were at address, then the clubface will not square up until it, too, is about six inches beyond the point where it was sitting squarely at address. The clubface can't catch up to the lateral drive and is still open when the ball is struck.

So you see, a lateral hip slide is a prime cause of the push-sliced shot. Not only does the ball finish far right of the target, but because the clubface is also open in relation to the path of the swing, the hit isn't square. So you lose distance as well as direction.

I can't emphasize too much the importance of making contact while the clubhead path is precisely on the target line, with the clubface pointing directly at the target. You have to hit the ball absolutely flush to maximize both your distance and direction. And to ensure that you can hit the ball flush, you have to give your hands plenty of room to release and square up that club.

You know, if you read a lot of golf instruction you may have the impression that most poor shots are a result of releasing the arms and hands too early so that power and accurate clubface delivery are lost. Actually, I think the opposite is true. Too many golfers don't release the club at all. Or at least, not at the instant of impact when it's needed. And I think a lot of it has to do with the fact that so many golfers slide rather than turn their hips through the downswing. It's not like they're saying, "I don't want to release the club so that I hit it long and straight." Heck, no. It's just that they're putting themselves in a position so far ahead of the ball that they can't release the arms, hands, and club the way they want to.

This is why the old image of "turning in a barrel" has really stood the test of time. It helps you transmit the power from your lower body into your upper body and finally the club, while at the same time keeping you in position to release the club freely through the impact zone.

Remember what I said earlier about the golf swing being one continuous turn. Just as you should turn to the maximum to the right on the backswing, you must keep turning to the left as much as you can while coming down. As long as you're making a circular turn rather than a sway toward the target, you'll be in great shape at impact.

HEAD BEHIND BALL FOR POWER

In your address position with the longer clubs, although your weight distribution between the feet is fifty-fifty, most of your weight will be behind the ball because, if you recall, the ball should be positioned virtually opposite your left heel. So if you drew a line straight up from the ball, your entire upper body, including your head, would be positioned behind the ball.

Now, if you can turn your lower body properly through the downswing, it should be easier for you to do what I want you to do with your head—which is nothing. Maintaining a head position behind the ball through impact is a key to powerful shotmaking—I'll explain why in a moment. For now I just want you to understand that having a relatively still head throughout the swing will allow you to be much more consistent in your shotmaking. I don't want you to make a stiff, tight swing by trying to keep your head in a vise, so to speak. Instead, I think it's easy to see that if you keep turning around a fixed center throughout the backswing and downswing, your head will stay pretty still. However, if you're driving your lower body at the target on the downswing, it's pretty darn hard to keep your head behind the ball. It will almost be forced to move forward with your hips, resulting in that lack of release that I mentioned earlier and mishit shots in general.

That aside, here's why maintaining that head position behind the ball will be a big help in maximizing your power off the tee: Doing so automatically helps you sweep the ball off the tee slightly on the upswing. And when you do that, the ball will carry and roll substantially farther than it would if you were to hit with a descending blow. The reason? When you hit down on the ball you impart backspin on it. Therefore, the ball starts off flying fairly low but then rises or "upshoots" later in its flight. Logically, it will then drop to the ground at a steep angle and won't roll far after landing. Conversely, when you sweep the ball, contacting it just as the club is moving upward, very little backspin is applied to the ball. Consequently, it zooms off the clubface and flies on a more even parabola, so that it lands at a shallower angle and rolls farther.

I'm willing to bet that if you have been hitting down on your tee shots, you'll add at least twenty yards to your tee shots by simply staying behind the ball on the downswing and hitting the ball on the upswing.

This super flight pattern with the driver is a direct result of keeping your head and upper body behind the ball at impact. Remember that the lowest point in your swing will always be opposite the center of gravity of your body. When your center of gravity stays behind the position of the golf ball, the lowest point in your swing will automatically be behind the ball as well. You won't have to make any particular effort to scoop at the ball to hit it on the upswing, but rather, it will happen naturally. (Incidentally, this is also why you may have noticed that the extra-long hitters usually tee the ball up pretty high with the driver. They stay behind the ball very well and contact it a little more on the upswing, making the hit as flush as possible to the loft angle of the clubface.)

So you see, everything works together in producing a powerful and accurate delivery of the clubface to the ball. You hit the ball a little on the upswing because you've kept your head and upper body behind it. You've been able to keep your head behind the ball because you made a nice full circular hip turn on the downswing rather than driving the hips laterally toward the target. That powerful unwinding action of the hips was triggered by the key first move of the downswing— slamming the left heel back onto the turf.

GO AFTER IT WITH ARMS AND HANDS

After you clear your hips, there's only one other thing I'd like you to keep in mind regarding the downswing: Feel free to go ahead and rip the club into the ball with your arms and hands.

Again, if you've read or watched a lot of golf instruction, you've probably heard that the hands and arms should remain passive through the impact zone. The reasoning is that if you've done everything right to this point, the centrifugal force you've built up will carry your hands and arms through the shot with no further effort from you.

Now, I've disagreed pretty darn strongly with a number of pieces of swing advice that you've heard previously. On this one, I'm also going to disagree, but not as strongly. It's true that if you've built up leverage through all the steps we've discussed, to a great degree your hands and arms will be carried along for the ride. They more or less have to hit the ball; they couldn't just stop of their own accord before impact.

However, I don't agree that you should be passive with your hands and arms through impact, for two reasons. First, as I've suggested earlier, I don't believe most club players are guilty of releasing the club too early from the top. Particularly among medium- to low-handicap amateurs, the more dominant fault is not getting a good free arm and hand release through impact. Second, I believe that given the proper sequence of motion and the buildup of power through that sequence, you will build more clubhead speed by actively utilizing each link in that chain, rather than by assuming that the link will work fully without your making it happen.

If that last sentence sounds as though I mean you should consciously rip the clubhead through impact with your forearms and hands, yes, that's exactly what I mean. Until just before impact, you've been pretty much passive with your hands and arms since starting the club away from the ball. You've used your body, not your hands, to generate tremendous force up to this point. Now it's time to make that last

link in the power chain work for you. To me, really whipping the club into the ball with my hands and wrists is a real treat, sort of like a dessert I've been waiting for. Don't be lazy at the bottom of the downswing. Go ahead and rip right through it with a full release of your hands and wrists.

I might add here that you should take this aggressive approach through impact on all your full shots, not just with the driver. I believe you should keep the full-swing principles the same for every club in the bag, unless you're in a situation in which the circumstances definitely call for a special type of shot.

But I really don't like to vary my swing pattern too much because consistency is really the name of this game. And in terms of shotmaking, you'll find that using my power swing will help you hit the ball much higher as well as longer than you ever have before. Hitting higher iron shots is an immediate benefit because it will allow you to drop the ball closer to the flag even when it's in a tight position.

THE FOLLOW-THROUGH: FULL AND BALANCED

Take a close look at the accompanying photographs of my swing, which show face-on and side views of my finish with the driver. One thing I think you'll immediately notice is that, although I might have just sent the ball away on a 350-yard flight, I'm in an extremely balanced and relaxed-looking position. There is no sense that any flailing, leaping, sliding, or any other unnatural moves that would affect good balance have occurred during the swing. You can't fake a good finish; a balanced end-of-the-swing position can only be a postscript to a swing that was totally in balance.

When you complete the swing, take inventory of your positions. Start by checking your left leg; it should be in a relatively upright, firm position with just a touch of flex in the knee. The left leg can only be upright in the finish if it stayed relatively straight rather than bowing out during the downswing. This firm left leg at the finish indicates that the hips have made a nice counterclockwise turn throughout the downswing, as opposed to the hard lateral drive that makes you feel like you're generating power but ultimately leads to poor balance and mishit shots.

Your weight at the finish should be planted almost completely on the heel of your left foot as the result of the full unwinding action of the hips. Just a tiny amount of weight should remain on your right toe, since your right foot has been pulled up and around by the force of the downswing hip turn.

Ideally your chest should be pointing to the left of the target. That's another result of a powerful downswing turn. As with the length of the backswing, how far the upper body turns into the finish will vary from individual to individual. You probably won't be able to turn into the finish as far as I do, and that's okay. It would be great if you can at least end up with your chest pointing directly at the target. This would indicate that you've made a full and vigorous body turn through the ball.

As with developing the fullest possible backswing as discussed in Chapter 2, the benefits of working out with a weighted club will show themselves in a fuller follow-through and finish as well. Slow, controlled swings with a substantially weighted club will help you gain extension through the ball and then gradually extend into a fuller finish position. Just as the extra weight in the head and shaft will actually stretch your muscles into a fuller backswing windup, so will they stretch your shoulders, torso, and hips to turn in the finish, at least to the point where your upper body faces the target.

In my swing, the hands finish behind the head. My hands are still loose and relaxed on the grip, so that the clubshaft extends around and almost faces the target. Your finish probably won't wrap the club so far around you. The clubhead will likely be hanging down more behind you than winding back in front of you. Again, that's okay as long as you've let your hands go as far as they can.

My relaxed finish proves that I made an *on-balance* power swing.

As a final thought on the downswing, I'd just like to encourage you by saying that as you work on the elements I've outlined, and also use the weighted club to improve your flexibility, you will develop a motion that is much more graceful, flowing, and powerful. And of course, you'll see a whole different kind of golf shot coming off your clubface, too. That's the point of all the efforts you are making. Trust me

when I say that you will have to practice your new technique diligently, but the gains in direction, distance, and scoring will be worth it to you many times over.

Now that your full swing is in place, let's walk over to the pitching and putting green. I want to show you how big hitters can have great touch, too!

DALY'S DOGMA

Plant Your Left Foot

In order for the downswing to be a perfectly timed chain reaction, you must replant your left heel as soon as you reach the top of the backswing. This is an unorthodox movement of the body, but doing the following drill daily will make it feel like second nature.

Stand on your right leg only and swing the club to the top. Pause for a split second. Next, replant your left foot on the ground, heel first, and then swing the club down. Finish the swing on your left foot only.

Give It a Belt

Because I stress the importance of replanting the left heel and clearing the left hip on the downswing, I don't want you to get the impression that the right side plays a passive role in the golf swing. On the contrary, once your left side triggers the downswing, it's the right side that must rotate briskly through the hit zone for your clubface to powerfully compress the ball.

To promote a good release, try to finish with your belt buckle or belly button facing the target.

Practice with a Broom

Leg drive on the downswing is probably the most overrated element of a good golf swing. In almost every pro/am I play in, I see evidence of this. The typical club golfer makes a good backswing, then drives his legs laterally toward the target. This lunge of the legs hinders the release of the hands-arms-club unit in the hitting area which causes the clubface to be open at impact. The result: a slice.

A drill that will force you to release the club properly with your hands is to swing ten times daily with a broom.

Cure for Your Hook

If your problem is hitting drives that fly on a severe right-to-left hook pattern, the clubface is definitely closing at impact. However, your swing may not be the root cause. It could be that one of the following two problems with your equipment is the root cause of your hook:

1. The grips on your clubs could be too thin, which means you'll exaggerate wrist action in the hitting area and close the clubface.

2. The shafts on your clubs could be too flexible, which means that the head of the club is flexing too far forward and closing the clubface in the impact zone.

Cure for Your Slice

If you're delivering the club into impact with an open face and hitting a slice with the driver, you might want to check with your local pro to see if your equipment is properly suited to your natural strengths and tendencies:

The shafts on your clubs might be too stiff for you, which means you lack the strength and clubhead speed to whip the clubface squarely into the ball.

The grips on your clubs might be too thick, which inhibits the releasing action of your hands and causes the clubface to be open at impact.

Yes, You Can Hit a One-Iron

A one-iron is one of the most useful driving clubs made. Actually it features more loft than the average one-wood, yet I bet if you polled golfers around the world, the one-iron would be their least favorite club.

In the past, I think amateur golfers were justified in fearing the one-iron; the old designs featured such a narrow clubface that even the pros called it the "knife."

Today, however, the one-iron features a large head and is sole weighted. Therefore, it is aesthetically more pleasing to the eye and easier to hit. My advice: If you don't have a one-iron, buy one that looks pleasing to your eye and feels good, because it will allow you to hit more narrow fairways and will thus save you vital strokes on the course.

Once you purchase a one-iron, go to the practice tee and do this drill: Tee up a dozen balls and hit six of them with a seven-iron if that's your favorite club. Then put the one-iron in your hand and pretend it is a seven-iron. Swing at the remaining six balls and prove to yourself that your problem was mostly in your head.

Clear the Way for the Club

In making the transition from the backswing to the downswing, many club-level golfers make the mistake of pulling the driver down hard with their hands. Pulling the club down is okay when playing a short iron shot from rough. But since a tee shot demands that you hit with a sweeping action, you must create a shallow angle of attack by rotating your hips to your left at the start of the downswing. This clearing action of the hips allows your arms to swing away from your body and whip the club powerfully through the ball.

High Tee

When hitting a driver, the club should contact the ball on the upswing. To encourage the necessary "uppercut" at impact, pretend that there is a second ball teed up extra high about an inch in front of the ball you are about to hit. Knock that forward ball off its perch and watch the one you hit sail off into the sunset.

4
HOW I HIT IT "SHORT"

The game of golf is truly an unbelievable challenge. That's why we all love it so much. Golf tests your coordination, muscular strength, and athletic ability; it tests your mental toughness and your ability to manage both your game and your emotions; and finally, it tests that indescribable element called "feel" or "touch" in the short game, an element that every champion must possess.

At the time of this writing, I haven't been on the "big circuit" that long, but I can tell you this for sure: You have to have your short game and your putting stroke in high gear if you expect to contend for titles on the PGA Tour. Nobody, not even I, can hit the ball so far and so straight, so much better than each of the other 149 guys in the field, that he can expect to win if his short game is just decent. That might not have been true when a guy like Ben Hogan was at his peak, but I assure you it is today.

Let me give you an example of why, even when I'm playing my absolute best, I need a great short game to back me up. In the 1991 PGA at very tough Crooked Stick, I had shot three straight rounds in the sixties and went into the final day with a three-stroke lead. It was early in the final round that I finally hit a couple of shaky shots (it happens to everybody in every tournament, even when you win, believe me). In retrospect, I'm sure a lot, if not all, of the huge gallery was starting to think, "Oh-oh, here it comes, Daly's going to choke after all."

Anyway, I hit a bad second shot on the long par-four fourth

hole. I found myself with a difficult lob out of PGA-style rough, over a pot bunker, then downhill on a lightning-quick green without much of it to work with. A mistake here could have meant double-bogey easy, and even if I played the shot decently, I would not be able to stop the ball close enough to have a reasonable chance at saving par. It wasn't a good situation.

However, I really do have a lot of confidence in my short game and particularly in the pop lobs around the green. In this case I lofted a nice little shot that slipped down the slope about eight feet past the hole. To the gallery, which is used to seeing us pros knock short shots very close to the hole, the result might have seemed just okay, but any fine golfer will tell you that from that position, it was a hell of a shot. It really gave me a boost and I proceeded to hole the putt. The crisis was past and I went on to build my lead back up again.

You probably won't have the chance to compete for a major championship, but there will be many occasions when a super short game will turn a close match in your favor. Let's face it, like me, you are going to have those days when your timing is a little off or you've temporarily crept into a faulty address position, so you're not hitting the ball your best. However, if you've got an ironclad short game, you'll know that you can still win matches or Nassau bets on your off days. That's a great feeling.

I would say that a top-notch short game is even more important in match play, at which most club events are held, than it is in stroke play. Let me tell you, an opponent who is getting the ball up and down from tough situations is the hardest guy in the world to beat at match play. It's not only because he is saving strokes, but he is unconsciously getting under his opponent's skin while he's doing it.

Say your opponent gets home on a par five with two great wood shots and wins the hole with a birdie. You kind of figure, oh, well, he deserved it. However, suppose your opponent on that same hole has hacked it all the way up the hole and lies there in the rough, twenty-five yards from the hole—then he pitches it in for birdie. You're walking off the green muttering, "That lucky S.O.B.! I make a good solid par and lose the hole to a guy who was never on the fairway!" Psychologically, this guy's got you.

I suggest that instead of being the victim of somebody else's great short game, you build your own. In this chapter I'll try to do just that by showing you my chipping, pitching, and sand shot techniques.

A FOOLPROOF SHORT CHIP SYSTEM

Let's start at a simple level by talking about short chip shots from just off the green—usually in the twenty- to forty-foot range. To begin with, if the green's not super-quick and there's not a huge amount of break, develop an attitude that you want to hole this shot. Why shouldn't you hole it? Just because the ball is a few feet off the green, most amateurs get in a mind-set of just hoping to hit it relatively close to the hole. The good short game player, on the other hand, knows when to pick his or her spots, and very definitely concentrates on knocking the ball into the cup.

Ray Floyd has presented the best example of this over the years on the PGA Tour. How many times have you watched an event on television where Floyd was contending, and on a short chip shot he'd first take out the pin—so you knew he was into holing it—then either do just that, or just burn the edge with it?

Again, unless it's an exceptionally tricky shot, Floyd is concentrating completely on holing it out. Once you get this kind of thinking in your head, it's really surprising how many times you'll do just that.

With this in mind, let's go back to your planning of the basic chip. Say you're four feet off the green with a good lie on short fringe, and thirty feet from the hole. Assuming there are no bumps or bad spots on the fringe in front of you, the first thing you should realize is that this is a "chip" you should putt. Always use the putter whenever the grass is short and dry so that the ball will roll over those first few feet

almost as if it were rolling over the close-cut grass of the green itself.

You won't need to make any adjustments at all to your normal putting stroke (which we will discuss in detail in the next chapter). The only thing that might make this shot any different from a normal putt is that, depending on the texture of the fringe grass, you may need to stroke the ball just a fraction harder than you would have if the ball were resting on the green. More often than not, when I'm putting the ball from just off the fringe, I don't even have to make any adjustments at all because the fringes are exceptionally smooth at PGA Tour events.

A good rule of thumb is that if the fringe between you and the edge of the green is such that you have to worry about how much harder you have to hit the ball than if you were putting on the green, then you know your best strategy is not to putt it at all. It's time then to go to my basic short chip technique.

I'd like to suggest that you consider trying my way of playing these short chips from just off the green. When I'm within, say, thirty to thirty-five feet of the hole and just off the green, and I've decided I can't putt the ball, there's only one club I chip with. That's my most lofted third wedge.

Now, I know that most books would tell you that you should pick out the club that will nudge the ball in the air

The *third* wedge is the club I almost always use around the greens.

over the fringe and just onto the green, then let the ball roll the rest of the way to the hole. This club would be anything from a lofted wedge all the way down to a six-iron.

Well, I believe that on these short chips, where you want to hole out, you should really get intimate with one club, and practice with it until you can chip blindfolded with it and still hole out your share. And your best bet is to go with the third wedge, or if you don't own one, your sand wedge. Yes, with a third wedge you will probably carry the ball a little farther onto the green than if you decided to chip the ball with, say, a seven-iron, and the ball will roll a little less. But what's the big deal about that? It doesn't matter how far the chip carries or how far it rolls, as long as it finishes in the cup or, at worst, in easy tap-in range. Besides, when you adopt my short chip technique, you will hit a lower-flighted chip than you'd expect with the third wedge anyway.

Take a look at the face-on, down-target, and up-target of my address position for the basic chip on pages 92–93. My stance is open, of course, to allow me to get a nice complete vision of my target, and my hold on the club is light and relaxed. Beyond that, the important point I want to make concerns my unorthodox ball position. The ball is opposite my right toe in a narrow stance, and my hands are well ahead so that the clubshaft is angled back rather than pointing straight down. Also, my weight is about seventy percent on my left side, and I keep it there throughout the stroke. The clubface is square to the line I must start my ball on in order to hole the chip.

The reason I like to play my chips from this ball-back position is that it's the most foolproof way to play the shot. You must strike the chip with a descending blow and that's always the best way to hit any chip shot. The execution is simple. Draw the club back with basically your arms only, then use a counterclockwise rotation of the hips to help you swing crisply through the ball. By playing the ball back and focusing on top of it, you ensure that your clubhead will hit the back of the ball while still on a descending path. Thus you have eliminated any chance of hitting a "fat" chip, that infuriating

"duffed" shot where the ball goes less than half the distance to the hole.

A second point about playing the ball back like this is that in doing so, you have delofted the club quite a bit, maybe by as much as ten degrees. So in reality, the third wedge is like a pitching wedge now. This means the ball will fly a bit lower and roll out more than you'd normally expect with this club.

Basically, by playing the third wedge from this ball-back position with a firm-wristed stroke, only two things can hap-

Seeing my chipping setup from these three angles will give you a good *feel* for what you have to do when facing a short greenside shot.

pen and both of them are pretty good. Let's say you have thirty-five feet to the hole with five feet of fringe. First, if you contact the ball perfectly, the ball will fly well into the air, carry just about half the distance to the hole, and roll the other half. Second, suppose you err a bit and catch the ball a little thin. Well, chances are you will still chip it stiff or maybe even hole it! You see, the great thing about hitting it thin is that the total distance of the chip remains about the same. Instead of flying 17.5 feet and rolling 17.5 feet, if you hit it

When looking at my chipping action from these two angles, note how I control the backswing action almost entirely with my *arms*.

thin the ball may carry only ten feet, but because it lands on the green at a much shallower angle, it'll roll much farther, making up the difference in footage to the cup.

By the way, that's another advantage to playing the short chip with the third wedge. Even if you thin the chip, the club has enough loft so that you will still carry the ball onto the green so that it gets its truest roll. If you're using different lofts with the idea that you'll land the ball just onto the putting surface, and then you hit it thin, the ball will land on the collar and probably pull up well short.

Take a few balls down to the practice green and work with your sand or third wedge on those short chips as I've described, and I think you'll become confident with it very quickly.

The only time I don't chip with the third wedge is when I face a long chip shot, with say at least fifty feet of green, and/or where the chip is pretty steeply uphill so that the ball will want to pull up quickly. For those longer chips, I will most often go with a pitching wedge and use exactly the same technique as on the short chip—weight on left foot, ball off

When playing chip shots, I rotate my hips in a *counterclockwise* direction on the downswing, to help me swing the club through the ball.

right toe, hands ahead, and clubface delofted so that at impact it actually carries the loft of an eight-iron. Again I make a nice, crisp, arm-dominated stroke and strike down sharply on the back of the ball.

LEARN THE LOB SHOT

There is no doubt in my mind that the ability to successfully play soft, high pitch shots from deep rough around the green is a must for anyone who wants to be called a good short game player. Its value can't be questioned, as in the example I gave you in the fourth round of the 1991 PGA.

The pitch from long rough, particularly if you have a bunker, mounds, or swales in front of you, is truly a trouble shot, as opposed to the basic chip in which getting it up and down should be a matter of course. Sure, on the lob from deep rough, you still want to get the ball up and down and even hole one out now and then, but I'm suggesting that the risks are usually higher. So you need both the right execution and plenty of confidence.

Before showing you how to play the shot, I'd like to suggest that you make things easy on yourself by getting a third wedge, if you don't own one already. This third wedge is great for two reasons. First, it has quite a bit more loft than your sand wedge, usually sixty degrees as opposed to fifty-five or fifty-six on the normal sand iron. You automatically have one more club of loft in your hand. Second, the design of the third wedge is a little different from the sand wedge and makes it easier to play from all types of lies. You see, the sand wedge is designed with a flange that has a fairly high degree of "bounce." This means that the trailing edge of the flange is lower than the leading edge. As we'll see, it's a tremendous help when playing from the sand. This bounce won't be a problem if the ball is sitting up in the rough, but when it's sitting down, it increases the chance of the club bouncing up at impact so that the ball ends up being bladed. The third wedge, meanwhile, has much less bounce built into the flange. Therefore, having a lofted wedge is a huge advantage, to get both maximum loft and maximum safety in playing the shot.

I've found through my playing experience that you have to alter your technique a little bit in playing the lob shot, and that it may also vary from shot to shot because there are all kinds of lies, carries, and pin positions you will encounter.

Let's talk about the basic lob first. This is where you have a shot of twenty to forty yards, the lie in the rough is normal with a little bit of cushion under it, and you have at least

twenty feet of green to work with. Really, everything is in your favor here to get it close. Address the ball from an open stance that's a couple of inches wider than for the chip shot. Instead of a square clubface position, open it slightly so it's pointing a little right of the target. This will help you to put a little bit of "cut" spin on the shot, which will help lift the ball out of the rough and make it stop quickly. Last, play the ball more forward, off your left toe, with your weight evenly balanced between the feet rather than favoring your left side.

When lobbing the ball from rough, you need to make a slightly more wristy, U-shaped swing path than on your chip shots. This steeper angle will allow the club to move through impact with a minimum chance of the grass catching the club-head and twisting it off line or worse, snuffing its momentum so the shot falls short.

To get this steeper path, move the club away from the ball with a combination of an arm swing and a gradual cocking of the wrists. Practice will help you determine how far to swing the club, but from my experience I can tell you that you'll need to make a longer, fuller backswing than you would think you might need from the given distance. That's because to start with, the wedge you're using has sixty degrees of loft and you've actually added a bit to this by opening up the face. In addition, you'll be cutting across the shot a bit. This reduces the yardage slightly, just as it would on a full shot. So in most cases you'll probably be making about a three-quarter backswing for the lob shot, even if you don't think you need to go that far.

From the top, use your wrists a little more actively, but still try to lead the club through the ball with the butt of your left hand leading the way. This will keep the clubface open through impact, as you want to pop the ball into the air quickly. Follow through rhythmically on this shot, about the same distance you took the club back. The ball should come out high and softly and land dead, with very little spin of any kind. It's a misconception to think you can really put "juice" or a high degree of backspin on the ball out of the rough. The best you can do is hit a very high shot, so that the ball drops to the green lifelessly and stops fairly quickly.

If you're lobbing to a level, normal-speed green, figure on landing the ball just ten feet short of the cup since with this high flight it won't roll far.

Practice this shot with your third wedge, making sure to use the swing motion I've advised, and pretty soon you'll start thinking that the standard lob is duck soup, just like the basic chip.

Of course, there will be times when you've got a bad lie in deep rough. That's when the lob becomes one of the toughest shots in the book. You need to use your head here as well as good technique. If you have a pretty ample amount of green to work with—say, twenty-five feet or more—you can still expect to hit the ball close. However, it pays to recognize the times when you might have to plan on playing the shot past the pin rather than hoping for a miracle recovery.

When the ball is sitting down in the rough, there are several adjustments you should make in your setup. First, address the ball in the center of your stance, rather than forward off the left toe. This will allow you to make the more descending blow that you need to dig the ball out of the heavy grass. Second, play the shot with the face of your third wedge square rather than open. This will reduce the chance that the club's flange might bounce into the ball, rather than allowing you to get the leading edge under that tight lie. Also, your stance should be just slightly open, less so than when you are playing the lob from a good lie.

These setup adjustments assure that you get the leading edge under the ball and also that the clubhead does not get snagged in the heavy grass before impact. Aside from these setup adjustments, execute the stroke with the same upright, wristy swing so that your club describes a deep, U-shaped arc. Hold on firmly with the left hand as you move through impact.

As far as the length of swing is concerned, you might be surprised to find that it will be a little shorter than for the lob from the good lie. That's because you're playing the shot with a square clubface and swing path with the hands slightly ahead, rather than an opened face and an outside-in swing path. So the ball must come out lower and run farther than with the cut lob.

Depending on the severity of the trouble between you and the green, you've got to build some cushion into where you land the ball on the green. That's because from these lies, sometimes the ball will come out nice and cleanly, and other times it will come out soft. You've got to be sure that if the shot does come out soft, it will still reach the putting surface on the fly. Then the shot will probably end up close. If it happens to come out hotter than you planned, well, the ball might end up twenty to twenty-five feet past the hole. That's the price you have to pay for safety on this tough shot, but I think it's worth it. And there's nothing that says you can't hole the putt coming back.

THE WEDGES: YOUR "TEN-," "ELEVEN-," AND "TWELVE-IRONS"

Let's move back to the outer limits of your shot game—full or nearly full wedge shots from the fairway. My maximum distance with the pitching wedge under normal conditions is about 135 yards, my top distance with the sand wedge is around 115 yards, and the most I can get out of my third wedge is 95 yards. Now, your top lines with these clubs are almost certain to be less. It's not really important how far you hit with these clubs, as long as you know exactly how far you hit with the pitching, sand, and third wedges, so that you select the right club to get the ball close.

I believe you should play your wedge pitches from the fairway just like you would your other short-iron shots. Just because these clubs aren't numbered like your other irons doesn't mean you need to play them any differently. Really, they are just extensions of your set of irons—they could just as easily be called a "ten-," "eleven-," and "twelve-iron," respectively. Thinking about them in this way (at least on full pitch shots) might help you remember to make a full, normal swing when you are at or near your full distance to the hole with these clubs.

WEDGE PLAY FROM THE FAIRWAY: MY TECHNIQUE

In setting up to play a wedge shot from the fairway, I position the ball right in the center of a narrow, slightly open stance. My hands are slightly ahead of the ball so that my left arm and the clubshaft form a straight line, and my weight favors my left side.

When playing a wedge from the fairway, it's critical that you set up with your hands *ahead* of the ball *(left)* and assume a narrow *open* stance *(right)*, as these elements of the address encourage you to hit down and through the shot.

Making a *long* swing will encourage you to hit a more aggressive wedge shot.

I use the same setup routine as for all full shots, and again I trigger the takeaway with a slight increase in grip pressure. Then I try to make virtually the exact same swing as I do with a driver or a long iron. The only difference, if any, is that my wrists are a touch firmer as I push the club back from the ball than they would be for the driver.

I believe in keeping the swing tempo as smooth and rhythmic as possible on every shot. As you can see in the top-of-swing photo with the third wedge, my clubhead has still gone back slightly beyond the parallel position. That's not as far back as I take the driver, but part of the reason for that is that the shaft of the third wedge is much shorter. The sheer length of the driver shaft helps carry it farther at the top of the backswing.

Unless you're playing a pitch in heavy wind conditions, I don't believe you should get fancy by trying to hit the ball low using a shorter, quicker swing. Simply set up according to my guidelines, swing to the top, then let the downswing happen. Because you've placed the ball farther back in your stance and kept your weight toward your left side, you'll automatically come into the ball from a steeper angle and strike it with a descending blow, nipping it, instead of sweeping it as you would do with the longer clubs. (See photos on pp. 104–105.) Therefore the ball will fly extra high and land with maximum backspin. This is a big advantage because you can go for just about any pin position when you hit the high, full, spinning wedge.

SAND PLAY IS SIMPLE

Well, it looks as though you've gone and done what ninety percent of all amateurs regret more than anything else (except maybe knocking it out of bounds). You've missed the green and hit the ball into a bunker. So you're thinking, "It's panic time! This round can fly out the window right now, with just a few unschooled swipes at it from the sand."

I think more high-handicap players get a case of the yips when facing bunker shots than they do on the putting green. It's so obvious to me from playing with pro/am partners every

Playing the ball *back* in your stance is what allows you to *(from left):* swing the wedge down on a sharp angle of attack; extract a small divot out of the fairway turf; and make a free, full finish.

Wednesday. And it's really such a waste, because most of the time greenside bunker shots are among the easiest in golf. Sure there are certain lies, lengths of shot, and pin positions that can make for a really challenging bunker shot, even for a Tour player. But about eighty percent of the time the greenside bunker shot is really an easy play. I hope you will believe that, because this belief is the first thing you must have in order to start playing the shot well.

I had this assurance when I found a greenside bunker on the third hole of the fourth round of the PGA Championship in 1991. As I mentioned earlier, I had started out the fourth round with a few loose shots and the approach to this green

was one of them. Although the lie in the bunker was good and the lip of the trap was no problem to carry, I had very little green to work with. Still, I wasn't worried at all. I just flicked the ball out with my L-wedge (I'll get into club selection from sand later), and it settled in there so close to the hole that a tap-in for par was a given. It was one of the best sand shots I've ever hit.

Remember how I told you about the lob from rough that I played on the next hole of that same round to about eight feet away? Now, *that* was a tough shot. In fact, any pro on the PGA Tour will tell you that when he misses a green, he'd rather be in a bunker than in tall rough. It's just a much more

Open your stance when setting up to play a standard sand shot.

predictable shot, once you have your technique in order and your mind in a confident focus.

Let's look at the basic sand shot. This is where your ball is anywhere from twenty-five to fifty feet from the hole and lying fairly well, meaning at least three-quarters of it is above the surface of the sand. The lie is relatively flat and the ball is far enough away from the lip that you don't have to get the shot up extra fast. As far as pin position is concerned, if the lie is good, I don't care if there isn't much green to work with, you've still got an easy shot because the right technique will put plenty of spin on the ball.

First, you'll want a stance that's open about twenty-five degrees to the target. You should also align your clubface open, pointing to the right of the hole, by about the same amount as your stance line points to the left. This sets up an outside-in swing path through the sand which, coupled with the open face, will impart a definite left-to-right sidespin on the ball which assures it will sit real soft when it lands.

Your weight should be fifty-fifty between the feet. The stance is narrow with the ball positioned opposite your left heel so that at address, your hands are just slightly ahead of the ball. Just as a reminder, make sure that you hover the clubhead above the sand, because touching any part of the

On most sand shots, you'll want to set the clubface *open* when addressing the ball.

hazard prior to making the swing will cost you a penalty stroke.

There are two ways to control the distance you hit your sand shots. One is to make the club impact the sand a little farther behind the ball for a short shot, or to hit closer to the ball when you need a longer carry. (You probably already know that for any standard sand shot, your club should impact the sand behind the ball rather than the ball itself.) The other way to control distance, and the one that I prefer, is to try to hit the sand the same distance behind the ball every time, and use the length of your swing to control the force imparted to the ball. So I try to hit the sand two inches behind the ball on all normal shots and I recommend you try to do the same. I think this is the simplest approach and the one that will breed the most confidence.

As to the swing itself, after four looks and three waggles, I take the club back in a fairly narrow upright arc and allow my wrists to cock the club upward fairly early in the backswing. In the photo shown here, I am playing a medium-short sand shot (about thirty-five feet) from a good lie in fairly firm sand. This means I don't have to generate a great deal of force, and that's the reason my club has only traveled back to just past the halfway position (clubshaft just beyond perpendicular to the ground). On the downswing, I focus very intently on that spot two inches behind the ball where I want the flange of the club to enter the sand.

Pull down pretty firmly with the last three fingers of your left hand, then try to follow an image of slicing a cut of sand out from under the ball. This will help keep the clubface open at impact, so that you get greater loft and cut spin on the shot. Because the clubhead will meet more resistance in hitting sand on a rather steep downward arc, your follow-through will be restricted, so that the club will finish more or less pointing at the target, rather than moving into the complete follow-through position as with a full shot. As long as you accelerate through the shot, this is perfectly normal. You don't have to concern yourself with the length of the follow-through.

The shorter the sand shot, the *shorter* the backswing you should employ.

Accelerating the club through the sand is what allows you to launch the ball softly over the bunker's lip *(left)* and toward the flag *(right)*.

If you face a longer or shorter sand shot than the example I've given, all you have to do is adjust the length of your swing while keeping everything else constant. For a shot of twenty-five feet, you probably won't have to take the club to the position where the clubshaft is virtually perpendicular to the ground. If it's a fifty- to sixty-foot bunker shot, you'll probably need to make a full-length swing.

Keep in mind also the degree of firmness or softness of the sand, which you will have determined as you settled into your stance. This will factor into your awareness of how full a swing you need to take. If the base is shallow, you don't need to generate quite as much force as normal because the flange will "bounce" a little more. There'll be less sand between club

and ball and thus less cushion to the shot. If the sand is very soft, more of it will stay between club and ball and the shot will come out a bit softer.

Once you understand the mechanics of the sand shot, it's just a matter of repeating the shot over and over until you can do it in your sleep. Take a bucket of balls into a practice bunker and spend some time playing basic sand shots. Play a game with yourself in which you must keep playing the shot until you've completed a reasonable goal—say, until you've hit at least five shots within three feet of the cup, or until you've holed one. Then vow to stay in that trap until you've done what you set out to do. This is the best way I know to improve your feel for the sand shot.

ODD-LIE BUNKER SHOTS

Let's take some time to go over some bunker situations that are a little out of the ordinary—well, okay, I guess you can refer to these as scary shots. But really, I don't think any sand shot is that scary. Once you have your basic sand shot down, it's just a matter of knowing what adjustment to make to that basic setup.

Take, for example, a situation in which you have a long bunker shot, say about sixty feet, where you don't think you can get the ball to the hole with your normal technique. Two simple adjustments are all you need. First, depending on how much more force you need, address the ball with the face of your sand wedge squarer to the target. By doing this you are subtracting some loft from the club as compared to the open position for the basic shot. Second, bring your stance closer to square to your target. By doing so, your shoulder line should also be more square to the target, and this means that, instead of a swing path that cuts sharply across the ball, your swing force will be more directly at the hole and thus the ball will travel farther.

Incidentally, this might be a good time to mention that I actually play the majority of my sand shots with my third wedge rather than the sand wedge. This is a little unusual. The reason is that on short- to medium-length bunker shots, I generate plenty of force to get the ball to the hole, and I like to take advantage of the extra loft that the third wedge gives me. On longer shots, say over fifty feet, I might drop back to the sand wedge so that I can get some added distance without changing my technique. However, I believe most of you will get the best results by using a sand club which not only will get you up to the hole easier, but also has a larger flange which makes the shot simpler to play.

Buried bunker lies are a big problem for most amateurs. I think that once you understand what you need to do, they won't be. The main thing you must accomplish is to get the leading edge of the club under the level of the ball, so that the sand pushes the ball forward and out.

Most of the adjustments you need to make are in the address position. Assume a stance that is closer to square than normal, while keeping the ball position normal. Then, depending on how deep the ball is buried, close the face of your sand wedge to a greater or lesser degree—the more buried, the more you close the face. The main reason for closing the face is that it gets the leading edge lower and eliminates the bounce on the rear of the flange. So the leading edge will dig into the sand more, as it needs to, rather than bouncing off the sand and hitting the top of the ball.

With this address change, go ahead and play the shot normally, aiming to contact the sand two inches behind the ball as normal.

You'll find that by closing the clubface the needed amount, the ball will come out of that buried lie a lot more easily than you'd think. The only problem is, it will come out much lower and with almost no backspin, so that it will run after landing. If you've got some green to work with, say twenty-five feet or more, you can still get it close. However, when the pin is tucked close to the bunker's lip, that's when you should avoid trying to get too fancy; make sure you get out, and see what you can do about making the putt coming back.

One final note on playing the buried lie: If you happen to own a third wedge, it can be a tremendous benefit in this shot, for two reasons. First, the third wedge usually has about five degrees more loft than your sand wedge, so you automatically get more loft on the shot out of a buried lie. Second, because the third wedge has much less bounce built into the flange than most sand wedges, it will tend to dig into the sand (and underneath the ball) more readily without the need to shut down the club and take any more loft off the clubface. The net result is that you can hit a much softer shot out of buried lies with the third wedge. It's a great tool to have.

Uphill and downhill lies are the two common bunker conditions in which you may have to adjust the distance you hit behind the ball. Basically, the more uphill the shot the shorter it will travel, and the more downhill, the farther it will go. Factor this into the amount of swing force you'll need for the

length of the shot, just as you would the hardness or softness of the sand.

If you have a longer uphill shot, you might first decide to square up the clubface and your stance to give you a little extra distance as described earlier. If you judge that you still may not be able to get it to the hole, this is where you might have to try to hit the sand a little closer to the ball than normal, one inch instead of two. This reduces the amount of cushion behind the ball so it flies farther.

Remember that this adjustment is one you should practice before trying in actual play, because you're now in the habit of hitting two inches behind the ball.

The same is true of the downhill shot. If it's very short, your first adjustment is to open the blade even wider than normal for more loft. However, you may still find that you'll hit the ball past the hole considerably, unless you put more cushion between club and ball. If this will be the case, even with a gentle, short swing motion, aim to make the club enter the sand three inches behind the ball and make the same U-shaped, wristy swing motion, with the feeling that you're slapping the club into the sand at the appropriate distance behind the ball.

Naturally, I want you to practice all types of shots so that you're ready for anything when you hit the golf course. And while I certainly want you to work on buried lie, uphill, and downhill bunker shots, I suggest you do so only after you have your basic sand shot technique down pat. Work on this basic shot until you can consistently hit the ball within six feet of the hole, and you'll be a fine sand player. Once you've accomplished that, work on your setup and swing adjustments for the unusual sand lies. Maybe you'll then be able to go from being a good sand player to being a great one.

Now that you've got the ball within holing distance, let's step onto the putting green and examine how to finish the job. After all, no fine player ever shoots low scores without putting well.

DALY'S DOGMA

CHIPPING

How to Control Distance

The inability to control distance on chip shots is one of the most common problems among weekend golfers. In most cases, this is due primarily to a fault at impact; the typical player contacts the top of the ball and not its back center portion and thus imparts too much overspin on it.

The root cause of this type of mishit is losing the flex in the knees when the club enters the impact zone. When the knees lift, the club lifts, thus hitting the top of the ball.

To lock your lower body in place, address the ball with your knees a little more flexed and turned inward.

How to Control Direction

If you hit the ball the proper distance but your direction is off, there is too much play in your grip. Either you are using the wrong style grip or the pressure in your right hand is too light.

To attain a more secure hold on the club, try the following:

1. Assume a reverse overlap grip by draping your left forefinger over the first three fingers of your right hand.

2. Grip a bit more firmly with all the fingers of your right hand.

How to Deal with Wet Conditions

In wet weather, the ball will not run as far once it hits the green. But that doesn't mean you have to abandon your normal stroke.

To deal with this seemingly troublesome course situation, simply use a less lofted club and stick to your normal setup and stroke. The decreased loft of the "weaker" iron will cause the ball to fly lower and roll faster, but it will roll to the hole instead of stopping short.

Spot On

The art of chipping not only demands mastery of a stroke, it demands that you take into consideration the speed and break of the green. Watch any pro and you'll see that he stares at a small area of green where he wants to land the ball. Depending on the slope of the green, this spot is either in line with the hole or to one side of it. Depending on the speed of the green, this spot is either close to the hole or farther away from it.

The next time you chip, plan on hitting your spot—and you'll hit the hole.

PITCHING

Prime Cut

If you face a short pitch and the pin is cut very close behind a bunker, you must impart extra backspin on the ball so that it bites once it lands on the green.

To accomplish your goal of stopping the ball quickly, you must hit a cut shot by:

1. Assuming an exaggerated open stance

2. Swinging the club outside the target line on the backswing

3. Swinging down across the target line coming through, while holding on more tightly with your left hand to delay the normal release of your hands through impact

The ball will fly high, move quietly from left to right, and sit down so quickly you'd think the green had been covered in tar.

Slow Down Tip

A smooth tempo is very important to successfully playing a soft lob shot around the green.

If you are one of those golfers who tends to lift up the club quickly at the start of the backswing, pull it down hard, and fly the ball over the green, this tip will help you slow down your swing: Simply count one (as you start the swing), two (as you swing to the top), three (as you start down), and four (as you follow through).

Backyard Practice Tip

Worrying about how close to the hole you will hit a pitch is the one factor that causes you to take your eyes off the ball and hit a poor shot.

To become less target-oriented and more swing-oriented, practice hitting pitch shots over a badminton net in your backyard. Then, when you are on the course, forget about the pin. If you carry the imaginary badminton net, you'll hit the ball close to the hole.

Fancy Footwork

If your pitch shots fall well short of your target, you are probably leaving your weight on your right side on the downswing. This is why you are hitting the ball too high and weak.

To give your pitch shots that added oomph, actively concentrate on rolling your weight to the toe of your left foot at the start of the downswing and onto the heel side of your shoe in the follow-through.

Stop the Shank Shot

When the movement of your body and the movement of the club are out of sync, you will often hit a shank—a shot that flies off the clubface at a right angle.

A shank results when you contact the ball with the hosel or shank of the club located near its neck. This hosel hit indicates that your swing path is out-to-in.

To promote the proper down-the-line hit on the sweet spot of the club, place a foot-long cardboard strip parallel to the target line and about three inches outside the ball. If you hit the cardboard before the ball, you'd better work on flattening your backswing—taking the club more inside the target line—as that will promote the correct downswing path.

Be a Divot Detective

If your pitch shots consistently finish left of your target, don't automatically start changing your swing; it could be a problem in your setup. To determine this, look at the divot you took out of the turf. If the divot is pointing well left of target and shallow, you'll know it's not your swing that's causing the pull. The problem is that you are playing the ball too far forward in your stance.

SAND PLAY

Get a Grip

When your ball lies in sand and the pin is cut close to the bunker lip nearest you, you must hit the ball higher than normal and impart extra spin on it. To do both these things, hold the club with your hands turned much more to the left than normal. As a checkpoint, the V formed by the thumb and forefinger of each hand should point to your chin.

This grip change will allow you to cut across the ball, take a fine cut of sand, and put a high degree of stop-spin on the ball.

Don't Look at the Ball

Concentrating too hard on the ball is a big reason why amateur golfers become tense in bunkers and end up hitting a bad shot.

When I'm faced with a normal sand shot, I forget about the

ball and focus on a spot about two inches behind it; that's where I want my club to contact the sand. Try copying me.

This mental key will ensure that you will always hit the sand first and never the ball—hitting the ball, ironically, is the worst thing you can do when playing out of a greenside bunker.

How to Deal with Wet Sand

The typical high-handicap golfer becomes confused when having to play a shot from wet sand, not knowing whether to hit closer or farther behind the ball. Just in case you are one of those who is confused, let me set you straight.

In wet sand the club will not make such a deep cut as when the sand is dry. Therefore, you need to slow the clubhead speed by hitting farther behind the ball—say, three inches instead of two.

Brush, Brush

Making a good turn of the upper body on the backswing and a fluid follow-through are two vital keys to recovering from greenside bunkers. The simplest way to make this happen is to brush your chin with your left shoulder on the backswing and your right shoulder under your chin on the downswing.

5

PUTT LIKE A CHAMPION

People often have the impression that I'm just a long knocker and that I've played as well as I have on the PGA Tour because I can outhit everybody. Sure, I agree that my length is quite an advantage; but I think I'm a pretty good putter, too. If you look at the statistical records, you'll see that among PGA Tour players, I rank in the lower fifty percent among Tour regulars during my first full year. However, statistics are often misleading. Remember, any newcomer on the Tour is seeing all these challenging greens for the first time, while many veterans have competed at a given tournament site ten times or more and played, say, fifty rounds there. They have a big edge in local knowledge. I think I am an excellent putter and that statistically I will get even better as I gain the experience that many of the veterans have.

Putting skill is the most important factor on the PGA Tour (and it's probably the most important factor in your weekend matches as well). There's nobody out here who truly hits his average tee shot a short distance, but more important, everybody is a pretty darn good shotmaker or they'd never last on the Tour. Tournaments are won by guys who hit the ball solidly and accurately, who reach the green in regulation maybe a little better than the average of the field—and hole pressure putts time after time. You just can't win big-time pro events if you're not putting well. Watch the guy who's hitting the ball the best in a given week, but putting so-so against the guy who's scrambling from tee to green and then holing every putt. The hot putter is the guy who will win every time.

People think I won the PGA Championship just because of my long driving, and it sure did help. But the real reason I won is because I had one of the best putting weeks of my life. I made a bunch of putts in the four- to six-foot range—some for birdies, but mostly for pars after chipping or hitting my first putt past the hole. At Crooked Stick, with those big undulating greens, I had a lot of long difficult first putts and they were really tough to stop close to the cup. So I had to make quite a few short pressure putts that week. But I was really calm and confident all four days of the championship and I guess it showed. People tell me it looked like I was starting to walk to pick the ball out of the hole before I'd finished my follow-through. I don't think that's quite true, but I did have a great deal of confidence that week. And true confidence can only stem from good mechanics, which in turn lead to making enough putts that you have a reason to feel confident.

I believe that anyone from age eight to eighty can learn to become an excellent putter. You can putt well whether you have just taken up the game or you've been playing for many years and, like a million other golfers, have decided that you are the worst putter in the world.

I will admit that if you are in the category of self-proclaimed world's worst putters, you may have a little more mental work to do than the novice who doesn't judge himself or herself as either good or bad. But you have to get it through your head that you are not cursed with some kind of voodoo spell that condemns you to putting poorly forever. There's no lid on the hole for anyone.

I believe there are four steps to good putting, and they are quite simple. Anyone can do these things. But you need to execute all four in order for the ball to drop in the hole consistently. These four steps are:

1. Reading the green properly so you know the line the putt will take to the hole

2. Aligning the putter squarely to the correct line you've read

3. Delivering the putter along the correct stroke path, one that's right along the target line to the hole

4. Keeping your putterface precisely square to the target line at impact

These points make up the simple geometry which makes the ball roll where you intend it to, accurately enough so that it rolls right into the hole. I think that after you read this chapter you'll agree that it's not that hard to work these putting fundamentals into a smooth, relaxed, flowing putting stroke that, with time, you will be able to repeat without any conscious thought. Let's take a look at these mechanics first, then weave them into a smooth, natural stroke.

MAKE THE RIGHT READ FIRST

If you don't make the right read on how your putt is going to roll and break (or not break), you're probably going to miss the hole, even if you employ a mechanically sound stroke. So making good reads is an integral part of good putting.

There's no secret formula for reading greens well. It's more a matter of staying alert and aware from the time your approach shot has hit the green until you set up over your putt. For example, as you approach the green, you should keep an eye out for the lay of the land surrounding the putting surface. In hilly areas, a green may be built into a sloping piece of land, for instance, with a left-to-right slope. The green itself may look flat to you, because it contrasts with the sloping ground around it. However, in most cases the green in reality will be sloping somewhat left-to-right also. It's hard to see this once you're on the green, but you can pick this type of information up as you approach the putting surface.

Once on the green, don't goof around with your playing partners while waiting to putt. Instead, focus on the line of your putt. You might immediately decide that the putt has some amount of left-to-right break to it. How steep is this left-to-right slope? Is it a constant left-to-right slope from your ball to the hole, or is part of the line of putt flat? Keep in mind that if you have a putt that's flat at the start with a break later along the line, the putt will break more than if the opposite condition is true—when the line slopes early but then flattens out around the hole. This is because early in the roll of the putt, the ball is rolling faster, with more energy, and will not be affected by the pull of gravity caused by any side slope. The effect of any slope will be much greater if it occurs nearer the hole, when the ball is slowing down and is thus much more susceptible to the force of gravity.

A key to reading greens is being able to judge their speed. A lot of people don't understand this, but being able to judge the speed is just as important in determining the amount of break in the green as it is in determining the actual strength of the stroke needed (which we'll get to shortly). You see, if a green is lightning-quick, a putt will break far more than a putt over the same amount of slope on a slow green.

Let me give you an example. Look at a twenty-foot breaking putt at Augusta National, site of the Masters. These greens probably have the toughest combination of slope and speed in the world. Then compare the same-length putt with the same degree of slope on a public course where the green hasn't been cut that day (and public courses tend to be slow in general). Let's say that on a Stimpmeter (a device used to measure green speed), the putt at Augusta National reads out at twelve, while the one on the slow public course green may read out at only five. You just will not believe how much difference there will be in the amount of break, even though the amount of slope is the same. On the slow green, the break might be just six inches, whereas at Augusta that same slope might produce a break of two and a half feet—five times as much! So, always keep in mind the speed at the course you are playing when figuring the amount of break in a putt.

Remember also that the grain of the green may affect the break (as well as the speed) of the putt, particularly if you putt on Bermuda grass surfaces. If you have a left-to-right putt and the grain is running left-to-right, the putt will break more than you'd think just from judging the slope. If the grain is right-to-left, the putt will probably break less than you think, or possibly it won't even break at all.

If the grain is against you, of course, you'll need to stroke the ball more firmly, and if it is with you, the ball will roll out a little more at the end, so you must stroke a little more gently.

Here's the best way to check for any grain direction in the grass: Look closely at the edge of the cup. If you see a ragged or ruffled edge, that's the side the grain is growing toward. If the ragged side is on the right of the hole, the putt will break a shade more to the right—and just the opposite if the ragged side is to the left.

As to judging the speed of roll itself, this is the most crucial part of reading a green. Most amateurs do put a pretty good effort into reading the line, but if they're way off on the speed, they'll never make the putt. That's because if you've hit it too hard for the line you've chosen, you'll hit the putt through the break so that it misses the hole on the high side (as well as runs well past). Conversely, if you read the speed incorrectly so that you stroke the ball too softly, the ball will finish well below the hole (as well as short). Either way, not only have you missed the putt, you've got a lot more work to do to make the second one.

So as you're reading the break on a putt, learn to marry your read of the break with the certain amount of force you want the ball to roll with. You'll make a heck of a lot more putts when the speed is right. If the ball is rolling fairly slowly, it has a much better chance of dropping than if it still has a real head of steam, so that it must hit the dead center in order to fall. On the other hand, if you're off on the speed so that the ball doesn't reach the hole, well, it definitely can't go in. And finally, when your line is a little off but you've judged the speed well, the ball will stop within "gimme" range so you've eliminated the chance of three-putting.

Judging the speed well is really a matter of concentrating intently and gaining as much experience as you can. There is no set formula for judging speed. However, you can learn a lot right on your course's practice green, assuming it has a fair amount of slope to it. Go to an area of it where there's

a fairly substantial slope and start by hitting some twenty-foot putts straight uphill. Next, go to the opposite side of the hole and stroke some downhill twenty-footers. If your green has even a moderate amount of speed, you'll quickly realize just how much difference there is in the amount of force needed from one putt to the other.

One last point about reading greens both for speed and for break: If it's at all possible, play as many courses in your area as you can, rather than always playing one course. Seeing a variety of surfaces and staying alert to all the factors I've mentioned can only sharpen your green-reading skills so that you know with confidence where you want to hit every putt.

ALIGN TO YOUR SPOT

Once you've made your read, your next step is to align the putterblade as accurately as possible along the starting line of putt that you've determined will carry the ball into the cup. If you've determined that the putt is dead straight, the putter-face should be aligned smack at the center of the hole. If you've read a ten-inch left-to-right break, you must aim your putterface ten inches left of the middle of the cup.

An awful lot of golfers have trouble lining up their putter correctly to the line they've selected. It must have to do with optical quirks that certain people may have, and since I'm sure not an eye doctor, I'm not going to try to explain them. However, some golfers, for various reasons, aim the putter far left or right of where they think they're aiming it. This means they'll have to make some kind of unconscious stroke adjustment to get the ball started on the line they want. Adjustments like this can only lead to a lot of inconsistency in the end.

My suggestion is that you take some time on the practice green to learn just how you are aligning the putterblade. Have a friend stand directly behind you and observe you hitting some straight ten-foot putts, to make sure you're aiming that blade dead center. If you're aiming either left or right of the hole, make the adjustment your observer says is necessary, then get the feel of making a square stroke to your target. If, say, you'd been aiming the blade to the right, you'd have to pull your putts for them to have a chance to drop. When you start aligning correctly, you'll need to develop the feel of a corresponding, square back-and-through stroke to deliver the ball consistently on line. Believe me, if you've been misaligning your putter and then subconsciously trying to push or pull your putts back on line, you'll find you can become much more consistent by getting off a square alignment start.

I think it's a good idea to have a friend take a close look at your alignment periodically, at least once a month. After you've checked on straight putts, have him or her check your blade alignment on putts with various amounts of break as well, making sure you're aligned the exact amount left or right of the center of the hole needed to carry the ball into the cup.

In my case, I have my caddie take a look at my putter alignment just about every day, after I've completed my round. It's really important and almost everybody overlooks this fundamental. Don't be one of the millions of golfers who lines up that putterblade incorrectly.

KEEP YOUR PATH ON TARGET

Maybe a slightly less important factor, but still one that no one can afford to overlook, is the path the putterhead takes as it moves through the stroke. I say it's less important because research has shown that the ball's direction will be affected most by the angle of the clubface at impact. The path the putter is moving on also will have some effect on the line of putt, but the effect is not quite as great as the effect of the putterface angle.

Still, the best way to be consistent is to have everything moving square to your determined line of putt. If your stroke path is off, it means that your putterblade would have to be off in the opposite direction. However, the blade shouldn't be off line by as far as the path is off line because, as I've said, the face angle has more of an effect than the path does.

It may sound like I'm trying to confuse you, but I'm not. The point I'm trying to make is that it is very confusing to try to make up for a mistake in your stroke path by adjusting the angle of the blade, or vice versa. Get both of them on target, all of the time.

The main problem I see regarding the stroke path, particularly for amateur golfers, is that on breaking putts, they don't keep the putter moving along the starting line of putt that the ball needs in order to take the break and drop in. There's a strong tendency to push or pull the blade, depending on how the putt breaks, so that the putter path is moving toward the hole rather than along the intended starting line. When you do instinctively move the putterblade along the path toward the hole, the ball will take the break later in its roll and carry it to the low side at the finish. This is a very common error among amateurs, which I guess is the reason why missing putts on the low side is also referred to as missing them on the "amateur" side.

Always keep a mental image in your mind of the starting line you'll need to get the ball moving along in order to continue the path necessary to carry it into the hole. On big breakers, it really helps to pick out a spot just a foot or two along the starting line of your putt, then align your putter to that spot. Then concentrate on making a stroke that moves squarely back and forth toward that starting spot. Don't let that stroke path leak toward the hole so that you wind up missing on the low side.

PUTTERFACE TO TARGET

As I mentioned earlier, the most important physical determinant of where the ball rolls is the angle of the clubface as it makes contact. If you've squared it at the address position as I've described, your chances of delivering it square at impact will be a heck of a lot better. Of course, how you deliver the

face at impact depends on the kind of stroking action you make.

I will give you the details of the putting setup and stroking action I recommend very shortly. For now I'd like to just point out that a stroke dominated by the arms and shoulders rather than the hands and wrists is the one most likely to keep the putterface on an angle square to the target line. For consistency's sake this is the kind of stroke you want to strive for. You want to move the putter back more or less directly along the target line, with the blade neither opening a whole lot on the backstroke, nor closing too much through impact or the follow-through. The more you keep the putter on line while taking it back and starting down to the ball, the greater the chance that at impact, it will be pointing right where you want it.

The putting stroke has sometimes been described as a miniature golf swing, and I guess that's one way of looking at it. However, this description implies that the putter should move inside the target line on the backstroke, with the putterface opening up quite a bit in relation to the target line. Conversely, it should then square up at impact before moving back inside the target line with the clubface closing after impact.

The key point I'd like to make is that, except on really long putts, the ideal putting stroke need not resemble the full swing in this way. This is because you don't need to generate very much force to roll the ball ten or twenty or even thirty feet. However, the need for accuracy is very great. So it's better to make a stroke that keeps both the putter path and the putter-blade as square as possible for as long as possible, in order to maximize the chances for accuracy at impact.

Having said that, let's take a close look at how I put these mechanics into motion in my putting stroke.

REVERSE OVERLAP GRIP FOR BEST FEEL

Let's begin your setup to the putt by examining your grip. I think that your grip needs will be a little different on the greens than they are on full shots. Whereas maximum security is paramount on full shots, you won't be swinging the putter with so much force that there's any danger of your losing control of the club. Having the best possible feel for the putterhead is what you're after. That's why I go with what is known as the "reverse overlap" grip, as do the majority of better players.

Take a good look at the accompanying photographs of my grip shown from two angles. This hold is called a *reverse overlap* because your left hand is overlapping the right (for right-handed players), whereas on the full swing, it's the little finger of your right hand that is overlapping (or interlocking) with your left hand. So in the putting grip your entire right hand is on the club handle.

Start by placing the last three fingers of your left hand on the club's grip, while keeping your left index finger pointed outward, away from it. Place your left thumb on the top-center of the shaft. Next, with that left index finger still extended, simply close the fingers of your right hand around the grip, with the little finger of your right hand just below the index finger of your left. Your right palm should fit snugly

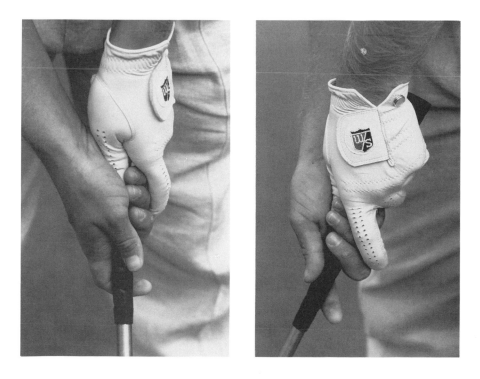

Studying my putting grip from these two angles will help you *clone* it more easily.

over your left thumb, with your right thumb placed at the top-left corner of the grip. To complete the grip, simply let your extended left index finger rest naturally over the fingers of your right hand, lying diagonally across them.

With the grip predominantly in the fingers and palm of your right hand, I think you'll agree that this putting grip gives you the best possible feel for the putter. Also, the right palm is in the best position to supply a pushing or pistonlike forward stroke of the putter that keeps the blade of the putter and the path of the stroke on the target line as we've discussed. (To enhance your feel for a push stroke, you might want to try crooking your right forefinger under the shaft as I do.)

THE SETUP

Once I've read the putt (which I usually do from behind the ball), I assume my grip as I'm stepping up to the ball from the left side.

The photograph on page 131 shows my putting address position from behind the ball. You'll notice that the imaginary lines across my feet, hips, and shoulders are admittedly a little left of the desired parallel-left setup position I discussed for the full shots in Chapter 1. Let me explain my reasoning for this slightly open setup position.

First, let me say that a parallel-left or square body alignment to the target with the putter is fine as far as I'm concerned. If you want to line up perfectly square, you're still in an excellent position to bring the putter back and forward along the target line, with no significant opening or closing of the blade itself. Tom Watson is one of the finest putters in history, and a good example of a player who has always used a perfectly square setup.

Let me tell you why I prefer to be a shade open in relation to the target. It's because I want to make sure that I make a solid stroke along the target line, while keeping my left wrist ahead of the putterblade through impact and beyond. In other

Standing a shade *open* when addressing a putt will help you make a more solid on-line stroke.

words, I want to make certain that there is absolutely no breakdown or "flippiness" of the hands and wrists through the ball. The stroke itself is a little more of a feeling of pushing the ball toward the hole, rather than using any kind of rotational movement of the hands around the body as we've seen in the full swing.

Now, if you are a little open to your target line at address, it more or less guarantees that you can make this square,

Here you get a good look at my putting setup from a face-on angle. Notice that I play the ball a bit *behind* my left heel and set my hands ahead of it.

pistonlike pushing stroke directly to the hole. You can also accomplish this from a square position. However, you can't really make a left-wrist-leading, no-breakdown stroke if you set up with your body closed, pointing to the right of the target. You see, from a closed position, you'd almost have to let your left wrist break down, so the clubface could close enough to deliver the putterblade on line to the target. Otherwise, you'd miss all your putts to the right.

So as far as your body alignment is concerned, you have a little leeway for personal preference. Either line up perfectly square (parallel left) to your target line, or line up a touch open to ensure a solid, pistonlike pushing movement toward the hole.

Let's have a look at my stroke setup from a face-on angle. I'm in a relaxed, comfortable position, using a fairly narrow stance, with my weight evenly distributed between the feet. Some excellent golfers putt from a stiffer, more cramped body position at address, the theory being that this type of setup forces you to stay still during the stroke. It may work for them, but I don't see the need for it. If anything, I think you're more likely to move from an uncomfortable position than you are from a comfortable one.

You'll notice that my hands are ahead of the clubface at address, with the shaft angled backward just a bit. I want to keep this hands-ahead-of-clubface relationship well into the follow-through and believe you should do the same.

I position the ball a bit behind my left heel, so that I contact the ball right at the bottom of my stroke. I believe that's the best place to make contact with the ball in order to hit solid putts. There are some teachers who advocate playing the ball more forward in the stance, off the left instep, so that you'll hit the ball a little on the upswing, in effect topping the ball to put more immediate overspin on it. I don't agree with this approach. I believe if you move the ball forward, it's much more likely that the left-wrist-leading-the-clubhead stroke will break down, disrupting that rock-solid alignment of the putterblade to your target. So find the spot in your stance where the stroke reaches its lowest point and play the ball from that spot.

MAKE A ONE-PIECE STROKE

The photograph on page 134 shows a face-on view of my backstroke. Notice that I've taken the club back with my

When putting, it's important to preserve the *triangle* formed by your shoulders, arms, and hands during the backswing.

hands, wrists, and arms all working as one single unit. That is, the triangle formed by my shoulders, arms, and hands has stayed in the same position, all moving in one unit to take the putterhead away from the ball.

In looking at the accompanying down-target photograph of my backstroke, note that the putterhead has moved directly along the target line back from the ball.

The player who swings the putterhead straight back along the *target line,* as I'm doing here, is the one who will consistently make square contact with the ball at impact.

I'd like to point out that this stroke is for a medium-length putt. You should try to maintain this solid triangle back-stroke on all short to medium-length putts. For putts of, say, thirty feet or more on a medium-speed green, I believe it's okay if you allow just a touch of wrist break at the top of the backstroke. That's because it can become difficult to maintain a perfect triangle on a long stroke without the action

Use a right-hand *pushing* action to control your putting downstroke.

becoming very stiff or "wooden."

From the top of the stroke, imagine your right hand as a piston that you want to pump right down your target line. Just push your right palm down that line, making sure that the slight backward angle at the back of your right wrist remains constant until well into the follow-through. Keeping the right wrist in this slightly bent-back position, with no

A *steady* head position will prevent you from pulling or pushing putts off line.

flippiness whatsoever, ensures that your left wrist will lead the way through impact and beyond.

Of course, you should keep your head still through and beyond impact as well. I mentioned earlier that some people have claimed that I start walking after the ball before I've finished putting it; well, those claims are a bunch of hogwash. I do start walking after my putts sooner than the next guy might, but that's not the same thing. Look over my stroke routine and you'll see that I'm really steady over the ball until the follow-through is completed.

If you feel you have a tendency to peek at the ball early and want to keep your head looking down at the spot where the ball was resting for a couple of extra seconds after it's gone, that's fine, too.

If I can make one more suggestion about the way you go about stroking your putts, I'd recommend that you don't spend too much time fretting over them. You should do all your prestroke reading carefully and deliberately, while others in your group are playing their putts. And, of course, you should set your putterblade along the intended line with great care. Once you've done that, though, I believe you'll putt better if you develop a routine that's relatively brief, then pull the trigger promptly. Too many golfers spend too much mental energy agonizing over what's about to happen, to the point where they have trouble drawing the blade back. These are the poor folks who are one step away from a sad case of the yips.

Stay loose over your putts and train yourself to think confidently about the upcoming stroke. Sure, the law of averages says you're going to miss more putts than you'll make, particularly from greater than ten feet. But if you work on the four key factors of putting that I described, then set up properly and always give it your best stroke with no second-guessing, I guarantee you'll make more putts over the long haul than a guy who turns every stroke into an epic drama. And you'll putt just as well twenty years from now, too.

Learn to savor and enjoy the challenge of the greens. Don't get too upset if you happen to three-putt a hole or two early in the round. Decide that the course owes you a couple of one-putts on the upcoming holes. With good mechanics, the right attitude will yield very satisfying results on the greens—and lower scores.

DALY'S DOGMA

Slope Solutions

If on putts that break severely you constantly leave the ball on the low side of the hole, change your ball position.

When facing a putt that breaks from left to right, play the ball off your left instep; this ensures that the putterface contacts the ball as it's almost closing and that you keep the ball on the high or "pro" side of the hole.

When playing a putt that breaks in the opposite direction, position the ball off your right instep; this ensures that the putterblade remains open and again that you keep the ball on the high side of the hole.

Get Some Shut-eye

Beginners are usually terrible putters, because they have no data stored in their brain about how the ball will react to a particular style and speed of stroke.

What I recommend you do in order to quickly learn how to gauge distance is to hit balls with your eyes closed. Before looking up, guess how far the ball rolled. In no time you'll be matching a stroke to a distance.

Plumb-bobbing Can Help You Read the Break in a Green

When putting, I don't recommend that you ever dilly-dally on the green. However, if you are perplexed as to how the green breaks, plumb-bobbing might help. Here's how it works:

Suspend the putter vertically at arm's length in front of you, holding the top of its grip end with your right thumb and forefinger. Obscure the ball with the lower part of the putter-shaft, then look straight ahead with your dominant eye (shut your other eye). If the shaft now appears to be to the left of the hole, the putt will break from left to right. If the shaft appears to be to the right of the hole, the putt breaks from right to left.

A Toe Hit Is Best on Slick Greens

When the average amateur golfer faces a downhill putt on exceedingly fast greens, he tends to shorten his stroke to try to compensate for the ball running more quickly down the slope. This is poor strategy because it causes you to make an aggressive slab stroke and hit the ball too hard.

The way to deal with this course situation is to address the ball off the less weighted toe of the club and contact it there, too, since that will automatically lighten the hit and soften the roll.

How to Win an Uphill Battle

In playing a severe uphill putt, guard against leaving the ball short of the hole by imagining that the hole is three feet farther away or by hitting the top of the ball so that you impart a touch of overspin on it.

Whistle to Relax

Although putting is the one stroke in golf that demands the least physical effort, it can be the most strenuous mentally, particularly when you have to sink a pressure putt to win the match.

At the 1992 Masters, I played with Fuzzy Zoeller during practice and during the actual tournament. Fuzzy whistles before he sets up to a putt because this relaxes his nerves.

The next time you think you are about to make a nervous stroke called a yip, whistle first and I bet you hole the putt.

Give Your Putts a Head Start

Lifting the putter on the takeaway is a common problem and one that leads to a chopping action at impact.

To promote a good follow-through and a pure roll of the ball on the greens, you must first start the club back low to the ground. The best way to encourage this low back take-away is to sole the putterhead two inches behind the ball and start your stroke from that position.

How to Deal with Wind

High winds can throw off your balance and thus play havoc with your putting stroke. To counter this condition, build a solid foundation for staying steady over the ball and making a smooth putting stroke by:

1. Widening your stance a few inches

2. Crouching over the ball more

3. Choking down on the putter

Adjusting for Afternoon Play

If you usually play golf in the afternoon, the greens will be markedly faster, owing to golfers having walked over them during the morning and the sun and wind drying them out. Allow for this increase in speed by making a slower stroke.

How to Make a Tension-free Stroke

The player who consistently leaves putts short of the hole is one who is overly tense. He presses the putter down into the green, holds the club with a death grip, and moves the putter back so slowly you'd think he'd been locked in a freezer for a few hours.

To promote a tension-free, arms-shoulders pendulum stroke, raise the putterhead about an inch off the ground and then start your stroke from that position.

How to Cure the Push and the Pull

Hitting putts either left or right of the hole may not necessarily be traced to bad body alignment or a bad stroke.

If you pull putts left of the hole, it could be that you're setting up with your hands behind the ball. If you push putts right of the hole, you could be setting your hands so far ahead of the ball that you force the putterface to look right of the target—exactly in the direction the ball rolls.

Have a friend check that your hands are either in line with the ball or a tad ahead of it.

How to Build Confidence

If you tend to miss short putts, it may be that the hole is causing you anxiety.

To cure this problem, practice the following for a week: Hit putts to tees placed in the green, two feet away from where you address the ball. The tee will take your mind off the hole, thereby allowing you to make a more relaxed, carefree stroke.

Furthermore, when you go back out on the course, the four-and-one-quarter-inch-diameter hole will look like a well.

Forefinger Finesse

If you're one of those golfers who will try anything, here's a unique putting tip that will help you judge distance better and stroke the ball on the correct line.

Instead of wrapping your right forefinger around the grip as you probably do when playing other shots, crook the tip of that finger under the grip.

I find this unorthodox hold very beneficial indeed, because my right forefinger is so sensitive that I use it to guide the putter on the backswing and downswing, and also to put the right amount of oomph into the hit.

About the Authors

John Andrisani is the senior editor of instruction at *Golf Magazine* and a former assistant editor of Britain's *Golf Illustrated* magazine.

Andrisani has coauthored three major instruction books with the game's top Tour pros: *Learning Golf: The Lyle Way,* with Sandy Lyle; *Natural Golf,* with Seve Ballesteros; and *101 Supershots,* with Chi Chi Rodriguez. He is also the coauthor of *The Golf Doctor;* the recently released *Hit It Hard!* with power hitter Mike Dunaway; and *Golf Your Way, An Encyclopedia of Instruction,* with teacher Phil Ritson.

Andrisani's popular instructional articles and humorous golf stories have appeared in golfing and nongolfing publications worldwide, including *Golf Germany* and *Playboy.*

A former holder of the American Golf Writer's Championship, Andrisani plays off a four-handicap at Lake Nona Golf Club in Orlando, Florida.

Andrisani was selected to appear in *Who's Who in America* for 1992.

Leonard Kamsler is a New York–based photographer whose work appears regularly in *Golf Magazine.*